O'er All The Weary World

O'er All The Weary World
Stories for Advent and Christmas

Sarah M. Foulger

RESOURCE *Publications* • Eugene, Oregon

O'ER ALL THE WEARY WORLD
Stories for Advent and Christmas

Copyright © 2015 Sarah M. Foulger. All rights reserved. Except for brief quotations in critical publications or reviews, no part of this book may be reproduced in any manner without prior written permission from the publisher. Write: Permissions. Wipf and Stock Publishers, 199 W. 8th Ave., Suite 3, Eugene, OR 97401.

Resource Publications
An Imprint of Wipf and Stock Publishers
199 W. 8th Ave., Suite 3
Eugene, OR 97401

www.wipfandstock.com

ISBN 13: 978-1-4982-1777-4

Manufactured in the U.S.A.   04/21/2015

All scripture quotations are from either the New Revised Standard Version, hereafter noted as NRSV, or the Common English Bible, hereafter noted as CEB.

New Revised Standard Version Bible, copyright 1989, Division of Christian Education of the National Council of the Churches of Christ in the United States of America. Used by permission. All rights reserved.

Scripture taken from the Common English Bible®, CEB® Copyright © 2010, 2011 by Common English Bible. ™ Used by permission. All rights reserved worldwide. The "CEB" and "Common English Bible" trademarks are registered in the United States Patent and Trademark Office by Common English Bible. Use of either trademark requires the permission of Common English Bible.

Dedication

I'VE FOUND THAT CHRISTMAS generally brings out the best in humanity, encouraging generosity of both spirit and substance. As a pastor serving Christian congregations for more than thirty-five years, I have been privileged to work with truly benevolent people. Church people, often the butt of jokes and the first to be called hypocrites, are among the kindest, least judgmental, most compassionate, generous, and forgiving people on the planet. I dedicate this book to my sisters and brothers in the church of Jesus, the lover and the healer. I embrace the whole wonderfully diverse world but I am particularly and unavoidably fond of those who are seeking to walk the way of Jesus.

"Blessed is the season which engages the whole world in a conspiracy of love."
—Hamilton Wright Mabie

Contents

1. Waking from Sleep | 1
   Romans 13:11–14

2. The Year Rose Reinvented Christmas | 11
   Psalm 72:1–19; Romans 15:1–13

3. Harriet's Angels | 19
   Psalm 146:5–10; James 5:7–10

4. Darwin's Evolution | 29
   Psalm 80:1–7

5. Ernie & Thankless Heathens | 43
   1 Corinthians 1:3–9

6. The Patience of PJ | 49
   2 Peter 3:8–15a

7. Aught of Joy | 57
   Psalm 126; 1 Thessalonians 5:16–24

8. Not Another Race of Creatures | 67
   Psalm 89:1–4, 19–26; Romans 16:25–27

9. A Humbled Heart | 79
   Psalm 25:1–10

Contents

10 Finn's Feast | 85
    Philippians 1:3–11

11 Gift of the Maggies | 95
    Isaiah 12:2–6; Philippians 4:4–7

12 Everybody's Got an Angle | 101
    Hebrews 10:5–10

13 It Is What It Is | 107
    Matthew 1:18–25

14 O'er All the Weary World | 115
    Galatians 6:2–10

15 Eben's Angel, a Children's Story | 123
    Luke 2:1–20

Preface

I AM GRATEFUL TO the many devoted readers of my first collection of Advent stories, *Yards of Purple,* originally published by United Church Press with a second edition published by Wipf and Stock. For years, some of you have been asking for more stories. Here they are at last. Although I have not included discussion questions in this collection, I hope you will use the stories for small-group conversations. Think about where God shows up as the story unfolds and imagine what you would do given each character's situation. This will lead to thought-provoking, soul-stretching questions.

These stories recount moments of enlightenment, decision, and revelation, moments to which we all, by the grace of God, have access. Many, but not all, of these stories take place in my home State of Maine because I love it so and it's what I know best. Two of the stories take place in Guatemala, a beautiful but troubled country that I have visited with two mission groups from the Congregational Church of Boothbay Harbor.

In these pages, angels often appear to let people know there is nothing to fear. Their appearances are supremely appropriate during the season of Advent. All but one story is related to scripture lessons traditionally celebrated during Advent and Christmas. The one oddball story, *O'er All the Weary World,* is based on a passage from St. Paul's letter to the Galatians. One year, in a moment of embarrassing but perhaps advantageous confusion, I read the wrong lectionary text. The name of that misfit story seems fitting as a title for the collection. I have also included a children's story

Preface

because, well, why not? Children are awesome. My hope is that these stories may provide you a source of grace and a reminder that we human beings are, in our best moments, capable of being true reflections of the holy One.

Acknowledgements

I AM UNENDINGLY GRATEFUL for my amazing family of teachers, doctors, engineers, and grandchildren. I love you all more than I can express. The acceptance, support, and laughter you provide are inestimable.

Special thanks to Marianne Reynolds, a woman of abiding faith and a talented editor, whom I am honored to call my friend.

Besides this, you know what time it is,

how it is now the moment for you to wake from sleep.

For salvation is nearer to us now than when we became believers;

the night is far gone, the day is near.

Let us then lay aside the works of darkness and put on the armor of light;

let us live honorably as in the day, not in reveling and drunkenness,

not in debauchery and licentiousness, not in quarreling and jealousy.

Instead, put on the Lord Jesus Christ,

and make no provision for the flesh, to gratify its desires.

—Romans 13:11–14, NRSV, A Reading for the First Sunday of Advent, Year A

1
Waking From Sleep

LOOKING OUT OVER THE glistening harbor from the private porch of her beautifully appointed room in the Anchor Inn, Nancy wondered why the "pay-back" idea had never occurred to her before. Why had she not, before this moment, thought of recreating the generosity of the mysterious Christmas benefactor from her childhood? Nancy's little brother, Malcolm, had called this person their "Mystery Santa." Actually, because young Malcolm had trouble with sibilants, it was "Mythtery Thanta." Nancy, however, had never believed in Thanta, not even when she was really little.

Nancy had always been a realist. She figured out, very early, that an actual person delivered a big red flannel bag filled with food and clothing and toys, making every Christmas possible for her financially-strapped family. The year she turned eleven, Nancy stayed up, and, while she was supposed to be tucked snugly into her frameless bed, she watched instead for this mysterious Santa. The entire Santa spy operation had been surprisingly easy. Her tiny bedroom window overlooked the apartment complex parking lot, equipped with bright streetlamps that stayed on all night. Just outside the door of her apartment building, two more luminous fixtures were mounted. From the darkness of her bedroom she knelt backwards on a wobbly ladder-back chair that was pushed up tight against the window sill. There she waited as patiently as an eleven-year-old girl can.

Even though Nancy didn't believe in Santa Claus or reindeer-drawn sleighs, she sort of expected a big jolly-looking man to show up driving a long fancy car. She was shocked when short scrawny Mrs. Johnson, who used to be her Sunday School teacher, got out of a beat-up battleship grey car. This least-likely of elves awkwardly lugged a giant red bag to Nancy's door. Nancy wondered how such a little woman could possibly haul such a huge bag. She was like one of those ants that somehow manage to carry leaves and insects ten times their size. Furthermore, it wasn't even the middle of the night. In fact, to Nancy's disappointment, it wasn't even ten-thirty. The threshold of her Christmas hopes, already low, just about bottomed out that night. And after that night, whenever Nancy saw Mrs. Johnson, she looked away, trying desperately not to reveal what she knew. She certainly did not want Mrs. Johnson to know that she had discovered her Christmas secret.

But that was a long time ago. Nancy, now thirty-two, a grown woman, wasn't poor any more- not rich, but definitely not poor. She worked in a biology lab in a big Boston university. She owned a spacious third-floor condominium in an up-and-coming neighborhood in Jamaica Plain. And she wasn't ever hungry any more. If Nancy never had to eat another peanut butter and cracker sandwich that would be just fine with her, thank you very much. Now, when she wanted a nice piece of salmon, she just bought it, the freshest piece of expensive Sockeye she could find. And now, when she needed a new coat or new shoes, she simply went out and bought them, not at any thrift shop, mind you, but right on Newbury Street if she liked.

Nancy spent her youth in a small second-floor subsidized apartment in Freeport, Maine with her father and little brother, Malcolm. It was an acceptable childhood, like an acceptable laboratory sample that serves its purpose, but being a poor kid in coastal Maine could be awfully painful. Of course, the other children in her apartment complex lived in the same low-income conditions as she but there many classmates seemed to have unlimited discretionary funds in their pockets and an endless assortment of nice clothes and good, straight teeth—kids who vacationed in the warm places in winter and attended interesting camps in the summer, things she and Malcolm never experienced.

Waking From Sleep

Nancy, Malcolm, and her father limped along year after year. She never indulged in pointless complaining. She learned from her father that a person could work very hard in this world and still be pitiably poor. What she needed, Nancy figured out early in life, was education. To that noble end, she worked diligently, became a high achiever in school, and won a few scholarships. In addition, blessed beyond belief in her sophomore year, an anonymous donor paid the rest of her college bills. Sometimes Nancy wondered if that kind and generous benefactor had been, once again, the petite and enigmatic Mrs. Johnson. It was surely possible. Her own father, God rest his soul, had worked interminable hours at carpentry and handiwork, but never earned quite enough to make ends meet let alone afford a college education.

The fanciest meals the family ate were the church pot-luck suppers. The nicest clothes she ever owned were hand-me-downs from the Haskell girls who lived down on the water in South Freeport. Nancy's best vacation took place the summer she turned 13. Her best friend, Marjory, invited her to Southport Island for a week to stay in her Aunt Maggie's summer cottage, a stone's throw from the ocean. She felt like a temporary princess that week. The lovely memory of that vacation helped her decide to come to the Boothbay peninsula again for a Thanksgiving weekend. She knew it would be a solitary holiday retreat but Nancy had grown accustomed to alone time. She was single, not by choice as much as by circumstance. Her brother, Malcolm, was married with two young children, a boy and a girl, but they lived in Oregon, too far to go for a long weekend. She would travel to Oregon for Christmas but for now, for the fine days following Thanksgiving, she gave herself a Maine retreat.

Nancy adored Boston and all it had to offer, especially its glorious book stores and aromatic cafes, but Maine would always be her home. Simply driving up through Maine opened a floodgate of thought-provoking memories. On the way to Boothbay, for old times' sake, she drove through Freeport, a village that had changed dramatically since she was a girl. She scarcely recognized the town crawling with tote-clutching consumers shopping black Friday sales. She did not bother to look for a parking spot but kept heading up Route One, eager to make the lovely right turn that would take her down ten miles of enchanting washboard landscape. When she arrived at last in Boothbay Harbor, it looked remarkably as she remembered. In the glow of Thanksgiving, she was grateful for so much, including little Mrs. Johnson with the big heart, so much on Nancy's mind.

As Nancy watched a lobster boat leave the Harbor, she wondered if Mrs. Johnson were still around. How could she find out? There must be thousands of Mrs. Johnsons in the State of Maine, perhaps dozens in the Freeport area alone. She could not remember Mrs. Johnson's first name. Was it Lucy? Laura? Linda? Perhaps she could call the Community Church in Freeport and someone might be able to help her. Nancy left her cozy room, went down to the front desk and asked the gracious Bed and Breakfast owner, Kathy for a Freeport phone directory. Suddenly, the idea of doing something appropriately thoughtful to repay Mrs. Johnson for her kindnesses consumed her.

"No more phone books," Kathy said as she pulled out a high-tech tablet and quickly found the phone number for the church in Freeport. With a sweet smile on her face, she wrote the number down on a little blue square of paper and handed it to Nancy, who took the information back to her room and placed the call. An older sounding gentleman answered the phone, identifying himself as Jack Wilson, the pastor. Nancy explained:

"I grew up attending your church, and I'm calling to see if one of my old Sunday School teachers still lives in the area. Her name is Mrs. Johnson."

Nancy described the petite woman with soft grey hair who wore big glasses and taught the third-grade Sunday School class for years.

Rev. Wilson answered, "You must mean Louise."

In that moment, Nancy remembered that her name was indeed Louise and her heart warmed.

"Louise Johnson," continued Rev. Wilson, "a dear saint in this community, died three years ago, right around this time of year as a matter of fact."

Nancy thanked the pastor for his help, but felt downhearted that she would not have an opportunity to thank Mrs. Johnson. She would never be able to give something back to this benevolent saint. Saint, Rev. Wilson called her. It fit.

A little sad that she could do nothing for Mrs. Johnson, Nancy determined she would get on with her day in the Harbor. At Kathy's suggestion, the first stop of the morning would be the Christmas Fair at the Congregational Church or, as Kathy called it, "The Congo Church". According to Kathy, the parking lot would be full and she suggested the five-minute walk to the church. So Nancy bundled up and walked through the charming town, making a mental note of shops she wanted to visit later in the day. The "Village Store," the "Smiling Cow," and "Sweet Bay Gifts" all looked especially interesting.

Nancy spent the short crisp walk contemplating ways she could return the favor of Louise Johnson's kindness. If only she knew of another little girl, one who was now living as she used to. That would be a way to thank Mrs. Johnson; she could pay her generosity forward. Not realizing that the main entrance of the church was down in the back near the parking lot, she opened one of the big main doors of the white clapboard church and stepped into a lovely meeting-house-style sanctuary with a red carpet, a fancy tin ceiling, and a grand pipe organ.

Nancy hadn't been to church in years. It felt a little bit like coming home and a little bit intimidating all at the same time. She saw a pile of folded papers at the end of the pew and picked one up. She sat down in the back pew and scanned the contents of the program for the upcoming Sunday's service, the sermon's title, "Waking from Sleep." Waking from sleep puzzled her. Beneath the sermon title, a passage from the Book of Romans was printed: "You know what time it is, how it is now the moment for you to wake from sleep." Well, in a sense this trip to Maine had awakened a dormant gratitude within her and a strong desire to do something for someone else even as others had been so good to her. Maybe this trip is a wake-up call, Nancy thought to herself.

And then it all began—as if she really had awakened from a busy self-interested life to a different way of looking, a different way of interpreting and responding, a way centered on others—the Mrs. Johnson way. Nancy stepped out of the sanctuary into an office area next to the sanctuary and saw a bulletin board. There, a big sign suggested that, as a Christmas gift, she could purchase twenty-five-dollars-worth of heating oil for a person or family in need this winter. Beneath the sign sat a stack of Christmas Cards on a card table. On the outside of each card was a pretty line drawing of a blazing hearth; on the inside were printed the words, "A gift of heating oil for someone in need has been made in your honor." Knowing how much the price of oil would be this winter, Nancy considered this a splendid idea. She took out her checkbook, wrote a check for fifty dollars, left it on the table, and took one of the cards. She would give it to Malcolm for Christmas, knowing he would appreciate this gift.

Nancy felt a rush of satisfaction and continued down the steps of the church following signs for the Fellowship Hall where she could hear the Christmas Fair well underway. Walking through a Sunday School area, down a light, freshly painted hall filled with lively children's artwork, she noticed another bulletin board. Another posted sign invited her to help the Sunday School purchase a Llama for a poor family in Bolivia through the Heifer Project. She wrote a check for twenty-five dollars, tacked it face down beneath the poster and, curiously, felt twenty-five pounds lighter. She noticed a brightly colored poster with a picture of a very Middle-Eastern looking Jesus with a bubble over his head that said, "Do unto others as you would have them do to you." Of course, Nancy realized afresh, the Mrs. Johnson way is the Jesus way.

She made her way into the church fellowship hall and found the place buzzing with people. They were slinging slices of fruit and cream pies, harvesting beautifully decorated Christmas cookies, displaying knitted hats, mittens, and hand-made ornaments, and offering gifts from around the world. But the part Nancy liked best was the silent auction. Six long tables were filled with interesting items—a stunning wooden bowl, sanded to a soft sheen, a pretty watercolor painting of the harbor, a basket filled with homemade blueberry and raspberry jams, a gorgeous heirloom doll with soft brown eyes and auburn tresses. Beside each item, a piece of paper was positioned on which to write a name and a bid.

Nancy bid on a tempting apple pie with a butter crumb topping and a magnificent toy pick-up truck crafted entirely of deciduous hardwoods, oak and maple and ash. Her father had taught her all about wood and Nancy knew he would have appreciated this fine work of art. She hoped for the pie but she pined for the truck. Though really too nice to be played with, she thought it would make a lovely gift for Malcolm's little boy.

She stayed for a bowl of delicious beef stew and, as she ate, she kept an eye on her potential prizes. Lots of people added their names to the pie list but the exquisite truck, Nancy was happy to see, attracted few bidders. A scruffy boy, similar in age to Malcolm's son, kept returning to the truck, looking longingly and running his likely sticky fingers around the wheels when he thought no one was looking. The boy's hair looked like a pile of stubborn weeds and he addressed his very runny nose with his right sleeve every few minutes. At one point, the boy's mother came over to distract him and seemed to be shaking her head "no." Nancy left her stew for a moment and wandered near enough to the truck to hear the mother say, "I'm sorry, Theo, that's more than we can spend today." "Pleathe, Mom," the boy begged, "Pleathe." Poor kid, thought Nancy with a smile, remembering Malcolm's childhood lisp.

After lunch, the winners of the auction were announced, one by one. The magnificent pie went to someone else, a disappointment but no surprise given the number of bidders, but the truck went to an elated Nancy who had been vigilant as a cat watching a goldfish in keeping her name at the bottom of the bid list. When she had paid for and picked up her prize, she looked around for the little boy but he had, apparently, left.

Nancy asked the woman who collected her money if she knew a little boy named Theo who had been at the Christmas Fair earlier. "No," replied the woman, "but I'm new around here. Let me ask Samantha. She knows everybody." Sure enough, the woman named Samantha knew young Theo who had wild hair, a pronounced lisp, and a runny nose, the very Theo who had coveted the handsome wooden truck.

"Would you be willing to make sure he gets this truck?" Nancy asked.

Samantha seemed not to know how to respond. An awkward silence followed, during which Nancy, getting ready to give up the truck, remembered the words, "You know what time it is, how it is now the moment for you to wake from sleep." Internally, she responded to those words, saying to herself, "This is a small start but I tend to wake up slowly."

Finally, the woman asked, "Are you sure you want Theo to have this truck?"

"Absolutely," Nancy answered, a gentle smile on her face.

"Shall I say who it is from?" Samantha inquired.

Smiling, she responded, "Tell him it's from . . . tell him it's from Mythtery Thanta. No, wait." Nancy stopped for a moment as if she had forgotten her own name, "Tell him . . . it's from Mrs. Johnson."

God, give your judgments to the king. Give your righteousness to the king's son.

Let him judge your people with righteousness and your poor ones with justice.

Let the mountains bring peace to the people; let the hills bring righteousness.

Let the king bring justice to people who are poor;

let him save the children of those who are needy.

Let it be so, because God delivers the needy who cry out, the poor, and those who have no helper.

He has compassion on the weak and the needy; he saves the lives of those who are in need.

—Psalm 72:1–4a, 12–13, CEB, A Reading for the Second Sunday of Advent, Year A

We who are powerful need to be patient with the weakness of those who don't have power, and not please ourselves. Each of us should please our neighbors for their good in order to build them up. Christ didn't please himself, but, as it is written, The insults of those who insulted you fell on me. Whatever was written in the past was written for our instruction so that we could have hope through endurance and through the encouragement of the scriptures. May the God of endurance and encouragement give you the same attitude toward each other, similar to Christ Jesus' attitude. That way you can glorify the God and Father of our Lord Jesus Christ together with one voice. So welcome each other, in the same way that Christ also welcomed you, for God's glory . . . May the God of hope fill you with all joy and peace in faith so that you overflow with hope by the power of the Holy Spirit.

—Romans 15:1–7, 13, CEB, A Reading for the Second Sunday of Advent, Year A

2
The Year Rose Reinvented Christmas

Rose's family thought her job a waste of her time, but Rose knew better. So did the many patients she cared for as if they were family. As a registered nurse, she would never see the sort of paychecks her brothers brought home, but Rose was drawn to her work as a cat is drawn to fresh cream. She could not imagine a higher calling. Furthermore, Rose believed her nursing career brought her far more happiness and satisfaction than her brothers' lucrative enterprises would ever bring them.

Rose's older brother, Frank, at the age of twenty-seven, owned his own very successful computer consulting business. On more than one occasion, he teased Rose with the word "loser," always extending the "ooo" as far as possible while creating an 'L' with his thumb and index finger and framing it mockingly on her forehead. She knew he thought this gesture funny, just part of the big brother job description, nudge-nudge, wink-wink, but this knowledge did not soften the slap of it.

Rose's oldest brother, Steve, almost thirty, was already an accomplished corporate attorney. With sickening concern in his eyes, Steve had recently told Rose that if she did not go back to school and get a real career, she was going to run out of time to return to school and start a "real" career. "You're the smart one, Rosie-O." She hated when he called her Rosie-O. "You could make a fortune with that brain of yours," he continued, "and every year you wait makes the possibility of the good life that much more remote." Steve was the master of the back-handed compliment. In the space of a few pointed sentences, he could make her feel like the humble little sister all over again. In her head, she came up with all manner of self-satisfying responses, such as, "You call working seventy hours a week protecting the big companies from the poor little people the good life?" But she said nothing. As the baby of the family, Rose was accustomed to being picked on. She knew she was supposed to let her brothers' criticisms evaporate on contact but, after twenty-five years, each word continued to sear her self-worth. Growing up, she sometimes imagined she must be adopted because she could not believe she shared the same DNA as these big oafs. Rose seemed to hold only one thing in common with Steve and Frank-their unmarried status. All three siblings were still quite single.

Her parents had paid for her nursing education with some reluctance. They, too, thought that she, the valedictorian of her high school class with near perfect SAT scores, should do something more gainful with her life. They never imagined she would actually become a nurse. Rather, they assumed it was a phase, one of those things idealistic young people do when they imagine they have the power to make the world a better place. But Rose's parents could not have been more wrong. For Rose, nursing was a passion, a mission that brought more meaning into her life than Steve and Frank would ever know. And based on her experiences, her nursing colleagues stood among the smartest, kindest, and most honest people she knew.

Almost three years ago, Rose started as a full time nurse in the oncology wing at Riverside Hospital and, regardless of what her family thought, Rose loved it. She loved the work, she loved her colleagues in the healing arts, and she loved the patients. Patients in her wing tended to be hospitalized for extended stays. For some, this period represented nothing more than a big bump in the road of life. For others, it marked the last earthly waypoint on the road to eternity. This Christmas season, her patients included Cole, a fifty-five year old man with a mysterious blood disorder on chemotherapy treatment; and Alfred, the sixty-seven year old Casa Nova of the unit, with scarcely enough energy to sit up and eat following a bone marrow transplant. Nevertheless, he charmed every female nurse who attended to his recovery; as well as Beryl, a woman close to his own age, who was fighting leukemia.

Riverside Hospital, regardless of the cheerful holiday decorations, descended into a deeper sadness in the weeks preceding Christmas. Patients received fewer family visitors as the demands of Christmas took them to Malls and obligatory parties. Strangers came around for a few minutes at a time, singing *Deck the Halls* and *Silent Night* from the safe distance of an outer hallway. But, this lovely musical gift made the reality of their hospitalizations all the more acute. Rose doted on her patients as a daughter or a kind sister to them all. In fact, she rather liked the idea that in some countries, nurses were referred to as sisters, a comforting title. In return, most of the time, her patients adored Rose and were grateful to her, even when she stuck them with needles, disturbed them in the middle of the night to check their vital signs and listen to their hearts and lungs. At Riverside Hospital, Rose was no loser.

She tried to bring a festive spirit into the oncology wing, to brighten up the place. She wore a blinking necklace of tiny Christmas lights. She draped and taped tinsel on the patients' I.V. poles. And when, about a week before Christmas, her patients started asking if she would be there on Christmas morning, she began to consider the possibility.

At first she figured the idea to be completely out of the question. Her parents probably would never agree to it and her brothers undoubtedly would offer a joint hissy fit. They looked like young men but, at Christmas, they turned into little boys all over again, clinging to the old childhood family traditions. As Christmas drew nearer, however, Rose really wanted to be at Riverside, perhaps to bring a little gift to each one of her beloved patients, certainly to sit with them, to comfort them, to bring a sliver of joy and perhaps even a sprinkle of hope into their often bleak and frightening situations.

Rose had nearly made up her mind when a conversation with the hospital chaplain confirmed her decision. Chaplain Richards spent a lot of time in her wing. Very often, he helped not only the patients and their families but also the nurses as they struggled with their own challenges and sorrows. Rose explained her dilemma to Chaplain Richards and, as expected, he offered no directive. . Instead, he encouraged her to search her heart. "And take a look at this," he said, handing her a Bible bookmarked to the fifteenth chapter of Romans. "We who are powerful," it said, "need to be patient with the weakness of those who don't have power, and not please ourselves. Each of us should please our neighbors for their good in order to build them up." The passage went on to speak of encouragement and hope. Rose knew where she was most needed on Christmas morning. If she could make this small sacrifice, surely her big strong brothers could too.

Her parents were surprisingly accommodating. They viewed Rose's request as an opportunity to sleep a little later on Christmas morning. From the days when Santa Claus was still a childhood fantasy in their home, the three siblings woke by five o'clock in the morning, checked to see that Santa's milk and cookies had been consumed, grabbed their respective Christmas stockings which had been, of course, hung by the chimney with late-night care, dumped the contents of the stockings onto the living room floor, stopped to compare loot and swap ogles, and proceeded to wake their parents with dramatic urgency. As young adults, the three children continued to reenact the early morning excitement with an energy surprisingly undiminished by their progressing years. And, although Rose was the only one who still lived at home, they all spent the night before Christmas in their childhood home and in their childhood beds with alarms set for 5:00 a.m.

Frank and Steve were incredulous. Why would their sister want to spend Christmas morning with a bunch of sick people? Wasn't Christmas supposed to be a break from work? Why would their Rosie-O suddenly overturn family tradition? Why would she sabotage their fun for the sake of some people who were knocking at death's door? They tried to talk her out of the ridiculous Riverside Hospital Christmas.

"Rosie, we promise you—these people won't care," they said.

"But *I* will," she replied.

"They want to be with their own families on Christmas," they argued.

"I'm the only family some of them will see this Christmas," she replied, instructing them to go ahead and open the stockings without her.

They accused her of trying to ruin Christmas. She told them they were acting like a couple of babies. They told her she belonged with her own family on Christmas. She told them that, as far as she was concerned, loving your neighbor came closer to the meaning of Christmas than waking up at an ungodly hour to see if Santa had done in the milk and cookies. They told her she was acting like a prune-y old church lady. Frank added, "That's fitting since you're well on your way to becoming an old maid." Steve pretended to be appalled by Frank's thoughtless and hurtful comment but Rose saw a fleeting wry smirk on his face. She wished she could come up with a snappy come-back but no male equivalent of "old maid" existed by which she might return the disparagement.

Women came in and out of Frank's life like magazines, about one a month. Steve had a long-term on-and-off relationship with another attorney, but both put more effort into advancing their careers than in settling down. Rose, a little plain and somewhat reserved, had not dated much, but was that reason enough for them to poke such fun at her? Did that justify their teasing? Would these brothers of hers ever grow up?

Rose tried not to care what they thought. At least, she tried not to care very much. She imagined she would enjoy Riverside on Christmas morning more than she would her callous siblings as they ripped wrapping paper from extravagant gifts they did not really need and could not well appreciate. Rose decided that a smile from any one of her struggling patients would mean ten times more to her than whatever expensive electronic gadget or sweater might show up with her name on it under the tree at home.

With or without their permission or approval, Rose was going to spend Christmas morning at Riverside Hospital. She was delighted to take the 24-hour shift that started at 7:00 on Christmas Eve. Her boss was very pleased as securing holiday coverage was always a challenge.

So it was that Rose started planning. She collected stocking stuffers, angel pens and rolls of lifesavers and colorful little packets of Kleenex. The other nurses chipped in, bringing puzzle books and miniature flashlights and candy canes dressed up like reindeer. Rose's remarkably supportive parents also contributed, buying small jars of jam and wrapping them in tissue paper and red and green ribbon. All of these things were tucked away in a closet in the staff conference room. Then Rose purchased fuzzy red stockings with fluffy white trim around the tops and stuffed them joyfully. The stockings were surprisingly full and she could hardly wait to play elf and, then, to see surprised looks on the weary faces of her Riverside patients. Two dozen stockings, Rose thought, ought to do it, since the hospital did it's very best to get patients home for Christmas. The only remaining patients were considered too dangerously ill to go home.

After a family dinner on Christmas Eve during which her brothers remained angry about her "inexplicable" break with tradition, Rose left. She had reinvented her own Christmas. Rose may have been the baby in the family but in this decision, she felt very grown up.

Patients' rooms in Riverside Hospital were very sad places indeed on the evening before Christmas. Old movies played on the televisions of patients who wanted to be almost anywhere else. But the next morning, on the day Christ is born afresh into human hearts, on the day when the birth of the one called the Great Physician is celebrated, Rose's patients did not disappoint. The unexpected stockings that had been slipped onto their beds as they slept thrilled them.

When she checked on Cole, he was laughing on the phone, undoubtedly with his wife, as a wind-up penguin from his stocking hopped about his bedside table. When she looked in on Alfred, he had convinced one of the prettiest nurses, Elyse, to help him solve a Sudoku puzzle from a book that had been in his stocking. Rose sat with pale, thin Beryl. Weak from disease and treatment, she needed help opening her stocking, help Rose was honored to supply. Rose's heart warmed once more by the decision she had made as that entire wing of Riverside became, at least for a little while, a glorious place of joy and hope, a place of building up neighbors. This is the good life, Rose reminded herself.

When Rose returned home, Christmas dinner was long over. Hers was the only stocking that still hung by the chimney. The others were on the floor, surrounded by crumpled bits and balls of Christmas wrapping paper and opened packages. Her brothers continued to be openly disdainful of her absence from the customary commotion. They did their best to convince her that she had missed the most outstanding Christmas crack-of-dawn ever, but their smirks and snipes did not work this time. They just couldn't get through to her now because Rose held a deep peace within her that surpassed their understanding. And perhaps for the first time in her life, this day truly felt like Christmas.

Happy are those whose help is the God of Jacob, whose hope is in the Lord their God,

who made heaven and earth, the sea, and all that is in them; who keeps faith forever;

who executes justice for the oppressed; who gives food to the hungry.

The Lord sets the prisoners free; the Lord opens the eyes of the blind.

The Lord lifts up those who are bowed down; the Lord loves the righteous.

The Lord watches over the strangers, upholds the orphan and the widow

but will bring the way of the wicked to ruin.

The Lord will reign forever, your God, O Zion, for all generations. Praise the Lord!

—Psalm 146:5–10, NRSV, A Reading for the Third Sunday of Advent, Year A

Be patient, therefore, beloved, until the coming of the Lord.

The farmer waits for the precious crop from the earth,

being patient with it until it receives the early and the late rains. You also must be patient.

Strengthen your hearts, for the coming of the Lord is near.

Beloved, do not grumble against one another, so that you may not be judged.

See, the Judge is standing at the doors!

As an example of suffering and patience, beloved,

take the prophets who spoke in the name of the Lord.

—James 5:7–10, NRSV, A Reading for the Third Sunday of Advent, Year A

3
Harriet's Angels

Harriet was always so blasted cheerful. While Jim struggled to read the morning newspaper, catching up on the latest skirmishes in Washington, the most recent projections for the stock market, the most up-to-date weather forecast and the most atrocious global-disaster-du jour, Harriet baked gingerbread angels and sang in the kitchen at the top of her lungs, "O Shepherds, aren't you happy? O Shepherds, aren't you happy? O Shepherds, aren't you happy?"[1] "Oh, pul-lease," Jim hollered brashly from his easy chair in the living room, "Can't you keep it down?" Harriet, fielding the complaint affably, turned down her song a notch to mezzo piano, but the unusual melody wafted its way, nevertheless, into the living room and Jim heard her continue, "O Angels, aren't you happy? O Angels, aren't you happy? O Angels, aren't you happy?"

"Harriet!" he yelled into the kitchen, piercingly, like a chef hollering to a waiter that an order is up. His wife stopped singing immediately but then, to his dismay, her silence was followed by footsteps approaching. "I can't help it," she said sweetly, now standing before him peering over his Wall Street Journal, "this old Shaker tune is spinning in my head like a dog who won't stop chasing its tail." She handed him a holly-dappled paper Christmas napkin wrapped around a warm fragrant angel cookie sprinkled with glistening crystalline sugar. Jim took a bite and nodded approvingly, but he did not smile. Jim rarely smiled. His nickname was

---

1. Shaker Text & Tune, arranged by several composers for choral use.

Grumpy. His closest friends called him Grumpy and he thought nothing of it. Harriet, however, called him *Mr.* Grumpy.

"I don't suppose many of those cookies are going to stay in this house," he sneered.

"A few," she said, "how many would you like?"

"*All* of them," he retorted.

"I'll save you a couple dozen," she answered kindly.

Every year in the weeks before Christmas, Harriet baked hundreds of gingerbread angels, bundled them into heavenly families in zip-lock bags, and brought them to people who needed cheering up. She delivered them to families that had fallen on hard times and to shut-ins who lived by themselves and to folks who struggled with various illnesses. Every year at the beginning of December, her pastor gave her a "special delivery" list, and she drove around distributing diminutive choruses of sweet angels to bring a bit of bliss into homes running short on joy.

She looked down into Jim's baby blue eyes as he proclaimed, "You *know* those shepherds and angels are happy! Why don't you ask *me* if *I'm* happy?"

"Oh, Mr. Grumpy," she said, bending down to kiss his shiny bald head, "I don't have to ask you that! I know you're not happy."

"I'd be happy if you'd stop singing and let me read my paper," he retorted.

"No, you wouldn't be," she challenged with a grin.

Jim knew his wife was, for better or worse, absolutely right. He had figured out years ago that he would never be Mr. Happy, Mr. Bubbly, Mr. Laugh-in-the-face-of-adversity. He wasn't sure why. Maybe too many disappointments as a child. Or perhaps 'grim' was simply his natural demeanor. Who knew? He supposed it didn't really matter why. This is who I am, he mused. And, in his own defense, Jim wasn't a totally miserable person; but, most of the time, he was not especially pleasant. That wasn't so bad, was it?

Jim benefitted from "opposites often attract," and he had attracted the buoyant Harriet, as merry as he was somber. He took her hand in his and, looking up into her benevolent brown eyes, he said, "Thank you, Sunshine," his nickname for her and he could conjure none more fitting. She was the light to his shadow, the sweet to his sour, the mirth to his dearth. Mr. Grumpy appreciated his good fortune of having married a woman who embodied sunlight. "What do you want for Christmas?" he asked affectionately.

"World peace," she answered immediately, as if the answer were completely obvious.

"Done," he said, "and what else?"

"The moon and the stars," she responded, her face beaming.

"They're yours," he added, "and what more?"

"Seriously?" she rejoined.

"Of course, seriously. No one is more serious than I. You know that."

"Yes, I do and so, what I really want for Christmas is for you to find something that will make you happy. Your happiness is what I want for Christmas."

"Humbug!" he answered.

"Well," she said, pulling her hand back, "you work on some ideas for being happy while I work on my cookies in the kitchen." She kissed him once more on that eggshell smooth head of his that she loved so well and bounced on out of the living room to continue her construction of angels.

What would make me happy? Jim wondered, so happy that my gladness would be visible to Harriet? What would make me happy enough to satisfy Harriet? Food was an obvious choice—a good T-bone steak and buttery mashed potatoes and green beans dripping with mushroom sauce—that could put a smile on his face! He could take her out for such a Christmas dinner. That would make him happy. This idea, however, seemed embarrassingly self-interested. A good football game, perhaps, a real nail-biter with the Patriots running the ball over the goal line in the last few seconds of the running clock to score the winning touchdown. That would make him at least temporarily happy but . . . it wouldn't necessarily make Harriet happy at the same time.

As he sat there mulling over Harriet's request, he found to his surprise that he missed her familiar high-spirited singing. But he couldn't bring himself to ask her to start up again after all his cranky clamor. Feeling a tad remorseful and unable to concentrate on the newspaper, Jim stomped off to put on some warmer clothes. The wood still needed stacking out back, and there was no time like the present. That's what his father always told him. "There's no time like the present," he would say severely when Jim had homework to finish or trash needed removing or the driveway, shoveling.

Jim always found stacking wood therapeutic in spite of the arthritis that had settled into his knees and shoulders in his retirement years. As he piled up the split logs, for some reason his giant jar of coins came to mind. For years, Jim had been saving coins in a two-gallon pickle jar, religiously tossing the change in his pockets into the waiting jar at the end of each day. Recently, the big pile of coins had overtaken the pickle jar and he'd had to find another vessel for his daily change. As he continued to load log upon leaden log, it occurred to him that he could put those old coins to work and perhaps *buy* himself some of that happiness Harriet wanted for him. Jim had noticed that, recently, his bank had placed a shiny new change counter in their lobby, the kind you pour your coins into for sorting. Like an old-fashioned slot machine, it makes a very satisfying ching ching ching as the change is mechanically sorted and electronically tallied. He could bring that big old jar into the bank and dump its contents into the change counter. Just watching all those coins turn into usable cash might make him happy for a few minutes.

Harriet came out into the back yard where the woodpile was starting to look downright organized. She'd come out there without her coat and had her arms wrapped tightly across her chest to mitigate the stinging cold. "I have an idea, Jim," she said.

"An idea that will make me happy?" he queried.

"Oh, no," she shook her head dismissively, "you're the only one who can figure out how to make yourself happy."

"What's your idea, then?" he grumbled.

"You—delivering these cookies with me this afternoon—that's my idea. If you drive, it'll go a lot quicker. You can leave the car running while I make the deliveries."

Quickly he reached for a viable excuse, "Uh, I was going to put some papers in order in the office this afternoon."

"Pretty please with sparkly sugar on top?" she pleaded as she shivered pitiably.

How could he say "no" to her?

"OK, I'll drive but can we stop at the bank? I have a little errand, Sunshine. It shouldn't take more than 10 minutes."

"Of course," she answered brightly and dashed back into the warm kitchen.

At about two o'clock that afternoon, Harriet was, at last, ready with her choirs of angels She had two big red plastic grocery bags, each layered inside with stacks of gingerbread angels. She brought with her a hand-written list of angel stops in a geographical order of sorts. Once in the car, Harriet said, "Thank you, Jim, this is a big help."

"Sure. Sure," he said in a very unconvincing tone of voice.

She lovingly placed a bright red Santa hat with cottony trim that had been stuffed in her coat pocket on Jim's head. "Is this really necessary?" he asked, looking in the visor mirror disdainfully. "It makes you look very handsome," she said flirtatiously. He started the car, staring ahead.

"Can we go to the bank first?" he asked.

"I *really* want to get this done," she implored. He surrendered wordlessly. "I promise, we'll be done before the bank closes," she added. He hoped so. He did not relish the idea of lugging the surprisingly heavy jar back into the house if they didn't make bank hours. The task moved along efficiently with Jim pulling up into the driveways of fortunate cookie beneficiaries and Harriet hopping out at each stop with beribboned zip-lock bags filled with agreeable angels. He watched as she knocked on each door, offered each gift with grace and compassion, and listened attentively as each recipient expressed heart-felt gratitude. Some of these folks had been receiving Harriet's angels for years. Many of them knew her well, and some refused to let her leave without a gentle hug or a kiss on the cheek. Jim observed his wife's yearly cookie pageant proceed, Harriet practically glowing with happiness. Clearly, what made Harriet happy was doing for others. "Doing for others; you don't suppose, he thought? Nah, it wouldn't work for me."

As they approached the next to the last stop, Harriet's cell phone rang. Her sister, Eliza, had experienced a terrible year—one surgery after another. Then, just a week ago, she suffered a little car accident, nothing too serious but one more rain cloud in a stormy year.

Jim pulled up into the driveway of the next stop. Harriet was utterly absorbed in the phone call. He looked down at his watch. 3:30. The bank would close at 4:00. How long would Harriet be on the phone? Sometimes, when these two got talking, they could go on for hours. Jim waved his hand in front of Harriet's face to get her attention and pointed dramatically to his watch. Harriet, in the thick of listening to her sister, smoothly slid the next zip-lock angel bag from her lap to Jim's and motioned with her free hand for him to walk up to the door and deliver the cookies himself. His eyes widened at the unpleasant thought and he mouthed the words, "Hell, no!" Harriet turned her head away deliberately and continued to listen intently to Eliza. Jim waited impatiently as three long minutes ticked by and finally, with an audible "Humph!" he got out of the car and marched up to the house with the blasted cookies.

The small poorly landscaped house clearly needed a paint job. He figured he could simply ring the doorbell and leave the cookies on the front stoop. Before he could put finger to button, however, a red-haired freckle-faced little boy flung wide the door. The five or possible six-year-old said, "Who are you? Santa?" Remembering the fuzzy hat that was covering his hairless head, Jim handed the question right back to him, saying, "No! Who are you?"

"I'm Jonathan. What's in the bag?"

"Cookies."

"Oh, I like cookies!" the boy announced with enthusiasm.

"Me too!" said Jim petulantly.

"Are they for you or for me?" Jonathan asked.

"They're for your mother," Jim replied.

"Oh," Jonathan said with disappointment,

"I'll go get her." The boy ran off and came right back holding the hand of a very tired-looking thin young woman with hair pulled back in a practical but most unbecoming fashion. "Hello, where's Harriet?" the young woman asked upon seeing the baked angels. Jim pointed to the car and held out the zip-lock bag to the woman almost as if it were a dirty diaper.

"Thank you," the woman said solicitously, but Jim turned around and left without so much as a "you're welcome".

He got back into his seatbelt without wasting any time. Harriet had, apparently, finished her conversation with Eliza, and he was greatly relieved. "What's *their* story?" he asked, motioning with his head up to the house where Jonathan was holding a cookie aloft like a trophy for Jim to see. Harriet answered, "Single Mom. Just lost her job. She struggled to make ends meet *before* she lost her job. They're not going to have much of a Christmas, that's for sure."

Jim looked at his watch again and tried not to think of the boy at the door. That boy brought back a memory, the childhood memory of discovering that his own father had lost his job. Several times, his father was "laid off" as they called it. And always, right before Christmas.

It was almost 3:45. "This is the last stop, right?" he asked, thinking about the bank and all those coins tumbling into the machine and the gratifying clinking noise they would make. He wondered how much was in there. Maybe $300. Or more! That would buy a little happiness. The next stop was, thankfully, right around the corner and went very quickly. With minutes to spare, Jim hauled the giant coin-laden pickle jar into the bank and headed right for the fantastic money machine. He put the jar down on the floor and took the lid off. He picked up the cumbersome cache of coins and then . . . he put it down again and secured the lid once more. As tellers closing up for the day looked on curiously, Jim marched back out to the car, put the heavy jar on the floor of the back seat again, and drove out of the bank parking lot.

"Is the coin counter not working?" Harriet asked.

"I'm going to a different coin counter."

"Oh?" Harriet wondered aloud. Jim did not respond. He simply drove right back to the house where Jonathan lived. Carrying the giant jar to the stoop, he dressed the top of it with his Santa hat, rang the doorbell, and ran like the devil to get back into the car before the boy showed up again.

Harriet shook her head and grinned all the way home. All she said was, "That was unexpected, Mr. Grumpy." Jim smiled a mischievous smile. He felt pretty good about leaving that jar of coins there. He envisioned Jonathan donning the over-sized hat and sorting the coins into piles, having the time of his life counting them. He could also well-imagine Jonathan's mother feeling like she'd hit a small jackpot and using that money to pay a couple of bills or to buy a Christmas present for her son or to go out and get a couple of T-bone steaks for their Christmas dinner. Identifying the prevailing feeling he was experiencing, the pleasing flush of his soul, Jim said, "You know, Sunshine, *that* made me happy."

"Merry Christmas," she said blissfully.

"*Happy* Christmas," he returned.

Later that evening, as Harriet was preparing dinner, Jim came into the well-tempered kitchen, wrapped his arms around her, and asked, "Why aren't you singing?" She smiled at her beloved, turned back to the gravy she was stirring, and continued,

"O angels, aren't you happy?

O angels, aren't you happy?

O, angels, aren't you happy?"

Shepherd of Israel, listen!

You, the one who leads Joseph as if he were a sheep.

You, who are enthroned upon the winged heavenly creatures.

Show yourself before Ephraim, Benjamin, and Manasseh!

Wake up your power! Come to save us! Restore us, God!

Make your face shine so that we can be saved!

Lord God of heavenly forces, how long will you fume against your people's prayer?

You've fed them bread made of tears; you've given them tears to drink three times over!

You've put us at odds with our neighbors; our enemies make fun of us.

Restore us, God of heavenly forces!

Make your face shine so that we can be saved!

—Psalm 80:1–7, CEB, A Reading for the Fourth Sunday of Advent, Year A

4
Darwin's Evolution

FOR DAYS, NEW YORK City residents fretted nervously over the menacing trajectory of Hurricane Sandy. The behemoth swirl of a storm seemed to be making a slow bee line for Manhattan. For a moment, Sandy flirted with the vulnerable outer banks of North Carolina but then her eye locked once more on New York. Forecasters pondered the merciful possibility that she would veer east and out to sea. But another recent storm had, at the last minute, taken the opposite approach, driving northwest into Vermont, destroying major roads and timeworn covered bridges and quaint homes in little villages that hadn't wrestled with a hurricane since 1938. Following days of increasing urban weather anxiety and coastal storm preparations, a determined Sandy was not drawn east or west; a direct hit on New York City was all but certain. Residents of low-lying areas of New Jersey, New York, and Connecticut were directed to evacuate.

Darwin and Julie were hunkered down, resting comfortably in their relatively secure Westside Midtown apartment up on the eighteenth floor with no worries about flooding. As the massive storm blew through the city, they could hear the winds pounding and the rains pelting. But they were never in any real danger. Darwin had taken the precaution of bringing in the cast iron table & chairs from their Hudson River-view balcony while Julie dug out flashlights and fresh batteries and dusted off a pretty glass oil lamp that hadn't been used since the great blackout of '03. Then, after their usual routine of evening reading, they slept surprisingly well.

All the while, Hurricane Sandy decimated the Jersey Shore, tore up Long Island beaches, flooded Staten Island neighborhoods and Connecticut shorelines, and used its terrible fourteen-foot surge to turn lower Manhattan into an unwitting Venice.

At six in the morning, Darwin slid out of bed quietly. Opening the balcony door, taking quick peeks left and right, he confirmed that he and Julie were not the only ones without power. Manhattan and New Jersey, as far as his darting eyes could see, were dark. The skies were still layered with rain-soaking clouds and the winds continued to blow forcefully but the center of the storm steadily lumbered away. Darwin could see that the Hudson River had risen over its banks impressively, completely covering Greenway Park. While Julie caught a few more winks, Darwin grabbed his yellow anorak, walked down the 18 flights of steps which were, he was glad to see, nicely lighted. The building's back-up generator was working. As he neared the bottom of the stairwell, he thought of the challenge of the eighteen flights back up.

"How are you this morning?" he asked the doorman, Tony.

"Tip top," Tony replied, "and you sir?"

"Never better," Darwin answered, repeating their daily script.

"You should have some galoshes out there this morning, sir," Tony added, the very word betraying his generational affiliation.

Darwin nodded and headed out into the rainy morning to see what Sandy had done. The neighborhood had been tossed about considerably—lines down, signs down, deep pools of water everywhere but he did not see any insurmountable damage. Darwin asked a police officer, "Do you know how the subways fared?" The officer told him that there had been some major flooding but the extent of the problem was as yet undetermined. Then he continued, "Your neighbors downtown have been flooded out."

"What do you mean?" Darwin queried.

"I mean they're flooded out. The only way you're going to get to Wall Street this morning is with a canoe and a paddle."

"Really!" exclaimed Darwin, trying to imagine this disastrous state of affairs. Once again Darwin felt grateful to be living where he did, on somewhat higher ground, not far from Lincoln Center. "Thanks again," he said to the Police Officer.

"Be careful," the officer replied, "you probably shouldn't be out there unless you have to be."

"Thanks," Darwin repeated and turned the corner to walk downtown. He needed to see the record-breaking flooding for himself.

Barricades prevented Darwin from getting too far into the mess but, from the buzz on the street, zone A was truly a disaster. Yesterday's streets, became today's canals filled with sunken cars and floating piles of debris. Wondering how to get a little closer, he spied a big unleashed dog heading in his direction. He quickly turned the corner to avoid encountering the unattended beast. Darwin appreciated dogs but from a distance; Dogs scared him, and they always seemed to sense it. Bitten as a child, he apparently never quite recovered. At sixty-three years old, he still feared dogs. He headed back to the safety of home, inwardly reprimanding himself for the phobia he could not seem to shake.

As Darwin hiked his soggy sneakers back up those eighteen flights of steps, he felt convinced that the subway was in serious trouble and wondered how he would get down to Brooklyn for his Tuesday morning class. Well, he supposed, he could always take a cab. Then Darwin felt guilty for focusing on the subway when so many people had undoubtedly lost their homes and livelihoods. Without question, he could live without the subway.

When he finally reached his floor again, he found Julie up and streaming news through her electronic notepad. She looked up when she heard the door open. "Did you bring any coffee?" she asked. Darwin laughed and shook his wet head, explaining that nothing was open down on the street. He told her what he'd seen and heard, and she shared with him the good news of their internet signal. Her notepad worked, and preliminary reports of damage were already posted on social networks. "A lot of homeless people out there," she said. "The Wilsons have started a network of temporary shelter. You can go right onto our apartment complex website and sign up to help."

This news did not surprise Darwin. The Wilsons were always out there doing good. You could count on the Wilsons to be on the frontlines of any neighborly assistance project. They served soup to the homeless once a week in their church. They mentored underprivileged elementary school students. They volunteered in the Upper East animal shelter. Last year, they adopted a mottled shelter mutt named Atlas, who, at any opportunity, barked at Darwin relentlessly. Joe and Mary Wilson's unfailing kindnesses pushed all of Darwin's guilt triggers, and he had plenty.

Darwin was the son of a Dutch Reformed Pastor. He grew up in a household of do-gooders and guilt-mongers. His father often seemed to care more about the rest of the world than he did about his own child, and his mother, though kind and attentive, demanded perfection. He never seemed to meet either of his parents' standards, and sometimes he felt he'd had enough Jesus in his childhood to last a lifetime. Allow a flood victim into their apartment? It was just the sort of thing his parents would have done. The pressure was on.

"Come on, Dar, we should offer to put somebody up. We have plenty of room," Julie argued. And that was true. Space in Manhattan came at a premium, and they were fortunate to own a double-sized apartment with a nice Master suite, a compact but well-appointed kitchen, an office, two cozy guest rooms, a second bath, and a living room large enough for Julie's grand piano. They could easily accommodate a temporarily homeless person or even a couple. Darwin's reluctance seemed to make Julie all the more determined and there was nothing new in that.

As he tried to conjure a good reason not to welcome a stranger into their home even though that stranger happened to be a hurricane refugee who may have lost everything in the floods and was probably feeling pretty distraught, his cell phone rang. His father, the Rev. William VanWijk, called to see how they had weathered the storm. "We're fine, Pop," Darwin answered, "Lower Manhattan is badly flooded, and I think the subway may be knocked out for a while. But we're fine."

Darwin's Evolution

"I'm glad to hear it," his father responded. Darwin could hear the genuine relief in his father's voice.

"Tell him we're taking in some flood victims," Julie piped up loud enough for Darwin's father to hear. Darwin held his hand over the transmitter end of his cell phone.

"Victim*s*?" Darwin whispered holding his hand over the phone and emphasizing the 's'. "What happened to victi*m*?" he added, emphasizing the 'm'.

"Tell him we're taking in a flood victi*m*," she repeated turning up the volume.

"What's going on?" William VanWijk asked his son, even though Darwin knew he had heard everything.

Oh, great, Darwin thought to himself. I've got Saint Dad in my right ear, the one who would fill his home with flood victims if he lived here and I have Julie in my left ear, who has somehow become the new head cheerleader for Hurricane Sandy Relief.

"Nothing, Pop," Darwin answered, "Nothing's going on. No power but we're fine. How are you?"

Darwin's Dad lived by himself in an elder-care complex in Pennsylvania. His wife, Darwin's mother, died almost five years ago after a long illness. The Rev. William VanWijk was still fairly self-sufficient. At the age of eighty-eight, he retained a car and a driver's license, though he seldom used them.

"Couldn't be better," Darwin's father said, "couldn't be better", as though repeating the words might make them more true. "Listen, son." How many times had Darwin heard these introductory words from his father: "Listen, son." The words were inevitably followed by fatherly advice. Darwin anticipated a measure of pithy advice about to be poured out upon him once more, like manna from heaven.

"Listen, son, let a little light shine on the situation. You'll know what to do."

"Thanks, Pop, good idea," and Darwin was pleased that the advice this time was both brief and generic.

Let a little light shine on the situation. Although a cliché,—light—light after a long night of darkness—light to see what could be done, what could be saved-seemed exactly suited to serve the needs of the hurricane victims. Of course, he knew his father didn't mean just any light. He meant God's light and Darwin believed others were praying for that, too, right now.

Darwin's parents chose this strong and unusual name because they wanted the world to know that God was perfectly capable of creating the universe in whatever fashion God wished. If that creative effort happened to employ an evolutionary path, well, that was fine with them. Furthermore, his parents, the Rev. VanWijk and the esteemed Susannah VanWijk prayed often that the human species would continue, by the grace of God, to evolve into the compassionate creatures they were divinely created to be.

His father had been a real force in his time and, of course, Darwin always felt the expectation that he would become a similarly impressive figure. Although Darwin had done quite well financially, he suspected that his lifetime of career hopping, from car sales to real estate to hedge fund management to teaching a few courses about the stock market at the University level, had disappointed his parents. His personal life pained them, too. He'd been married twice, no children, and now cohabited with Julie because he dreaded tying the knot again.

His force of a father had just said to him, "You'll know what to do." Darwin appreciated the unanticipated confidence that attended those words. And, in the end, those words contained the light he needed. Darwin already knew what they would do.

"Thanks, Pop. Now, is there a word for the day?"

"Well, of course!" he answered brightly.

With each phone call, Darwin's father, who knew his beloved son never set foot in a Church anymore, always offered him a bit of wisdom from the scriptures. For many years, Darwin tolerated this habit but, more recently, he looked forward to it. And he knew that, at some point in the not-too-distant future when his father was gone, he would miss it.

"I think I have a perfect word for today," Rev. VanWijk began, "It's from the Psalms, the eightieth. Darwin. Think about the millions of people affected by this hurricane and imagine them praying this Psalm. Ready?"

"Go for it, Pop."

And in that deep rich voice that had filled a big pulpit for so many years, VanWijk read, "Psalm 80, a prayer for Israel's restoration, greatly abridged:

Shepherd of Israel, listen! You, who are enthroned upon the winged heavenly creatures.

Show yourself! Wake up your power! Come to save us! Restore us, God!

Make your face shine so that we can be saved!

"That's good, Pop." And it was good and beautiful, this idea of God's facing shining upon a desperate people even as they prayed for help.

Darwin ended the conversation with his father, knowing that the right thing to do on this day of urgent and unprecedented need was to help however he could. As a very private person, the idea of strangers staying in their apartment unsettled him, but he also knew it would probably last only a day or two. Surely, he could manage that. Julie volunteered a guest room on their building's website and checked the box that indicated one guest.

Together, they put fresh sheets on the queen bed in the front guest room, dusted the furnishings a bit, and retrieved a clean folded towel from the linen closet. They had fun wondering who their guest might be—perhaps a famous New York author or an up-and-coming musician or artist. Feeling ready enough, they went back to Julie's electronic notepad and, while they nibbled on cold leftover chicken which they knew would not last long in a refrigerator without power, they looked at incoming photos. People waded through their neighborhoods hip high in flood waters, and rescue workers paddled through the mess in rubber inflatables. Photographs of distraught loss-stricken faces, shocking pictures of waterfalls cascading into plazas and subway tunnels filled the screen. Frightening video clips of houses being washed away along the Jersey shore as if they were nothing more than fruit crates displayed the storm's uncommon strength.

O'er All the Weary World

A knock at the door brought Julie and Darwin to their feet. For a variety of reasons, it could not possibly be their guest already. Their apartment building's strict policy required all visitors be received and formally announced by the doorman. Also, it was too quick. Only a few hours had passed since they had bravely offered to take someone in. Opening the door, they found their sainted neighbor, Mary Wilson, holding a big recycled shopping bag. Mary had an uncertain smile on her face, as if something might have gone wrong.

Something had gone wrong. Behind Mary stood a weary looking couple probably 30 years younger than they. Both had dark hair and thin faces, and the woman had striking light brown eyes. Behind them stood two children, two little raven-haired girls who looked very much like their petite mother. Sandwiched between the parents and children, sat a big blond hairy beast that looked for all the world like a dog. Julie's eyes were cast uncomfortably on the children; Darwin's eyes were fixed in terror on the beast. They were speechless and, if ever there were a contest to find the most convincingly inhospitable facial expression, both Darwin and Julie would have been runners-up that day.

Mary broke the uneasy silence, "Darwin, Julie, let me introduce you to the Margas—Marius and Christina and their six-year old daughters, Anna and Alina. And I believe this is Dragon, their dog—very sweet."

"Dragoi," one of the little girls piped up sweetly.

"Thank you very much for this," Marius Margas said, dipping his head humbly. There was a hint of an accent. Eastern European, Darwin guessed. Second-generation perhaps. One of the girls tugged on her mother's coat anxiously and whispered, "Mommy, I want to go home." Darwin grew up being dragged into the homes of strange and not always welcoming church members. One year, when he was ten, he was forced to play the part of the innkeeper in the annual Christmas pageant. He still held some residual childhood misery about having to pronounce the harsh words, "There is no room in the Inn." He snapped out of his shock, got down on his knees and said warmly, "Welcome. Is it Anna?"

"No, I'm Alina," she answered quietly.

"You're silly," the other girl said looking up into Darwin's friendly eyes, "*I'm* Anna."

"Are you twins?" he asked. The girls looked at each other as if trying to decide whether or not they should share their secret. They nodded at Darwin as their parents looked on cautiously.

"Do you like to draw?" Darwin asked, "I have some colored pens and some really nice drawing paper."

The dog growled at him defensively. Darwin stood up and stepped back. Mary Wilson had taken charge of settling a whole list of storm refugees into their apartment complex and was eager to move things along. When she suggested they all go inside the apartment, Julie was stunned. Still speechless, she wrestled with her anxieties around children visiting her apartment. Not really equipped for children, their apartment was the very antithesis of child-friendly. Julie treasured her breakable antiques, irreplaceable mahogany furnishings and, of course her magnificent piano

She was fine with the dog. Julie loved dogs. She grew up with dogs. She understood dogs. She'd always had a dog until Darwin came into her life. But children were another matter altogether. Julie imagined sticky fingers on her Steinway, small curious hands pulling first editions from her bookshelves and voracious little mouths devouring the wrapped Belgian chocolates from a Tiffany bowl in the middle of the dining room table. They needed a plan and they needed one fast. They had to find a way to locate more appropriate temporary shelter for this family.

Mary Wilson ignored Julie and Darwin's obvious anxiety, confidently shepherding the Margas family into the apartment. Julie pulled Darwin back into the hallway. "I'll take the dog; you take the kids," she murmured.

"Remember, this was your idea, Jules," he mumbled back.

"Surely, the Wilsons can find a more suitable place for them to stay," she added.

The Margas family didn't have much with them. Hastily evacuated from their home into a nearby elementary school turned make-shift storm-sufferers processing center, they were not permitted to go anywhere near their neighborhood. What they did not know then but would soon learn would confirm their worst fears: the home they'd worked so hard to buy and make their own was gone, along with many of the shoreline homes in their neighborhood.

"We're working on getting you some more clothes," Mary told the family. "In the meantime, perhaps you can get them settled," she said to Julie and Darwin. "Oh, I have some toiletries," and she pulled out of her shopping bag four zip lock bags filled with toothbrushes and soap and Band-Aids and washcloths and other useful items. To Darwin's great relief, Mary added, "Why don't I take Dragoi across the hall for a little while. He can play with Atlas. They'll have a great time. I'll bring him back in a couple of hours." Darwin was ever so grateful. Everyone knew about his issues with dogs.

The second guest bedroom was relatively clean, but needed sheets and towels. As soon as Julie emerged with a pile of linens, the family took all of this upon themselves, quickly making up the twin beds and getting things organized as if they were professionals in the hospitality industry. In short order, Darwin and Julie would learn they were indeed professionals. The Margases had their own housecleaning business, a small company that had grown very quickly. Their more than one hundred employees cleaned homes throughout the New York Metropolitan area. Soon they were calling from their cell phones, attending to business and trying to get through to their insurance company.

Darwin followed through on his initial suggestion to the girls, getting out a beer stein filled with colorful felt-tipped pens and a pad of large drawing paper. Anna and Alina immediately started drawing pictures of themselves in their home. Clearly, home was where they wanted to be. Darwin thought about the trauma of having to leave home in such a hurry and how frightened the girls must be. With a fat black marker, Alina took a second sheet of paper and started drawing the hurricane, the "stupid" hurricane as she called it.

The next two nights and days proved both awful and amazing, enlightening and inspiring. Julie walked with Christina and

Dragoi, a remarkably patient climber of eighteen flights of steps several times a day. Darwin continued to keep his distance from the dog, but he did seem to make some peace with the beast that, after the first night, stopped growling at him. Marius and Christina did what they could to keep their business going, and they seemed to take the news of the demise of their house with an admirable strength and calm. Julie and Darwin wondered if they could summon such courage if roles were reversed.

Anna and Alina tried to comprehend that all of their things were really and truly gone. From time to time, each girl would come up with a fresh version of the same question and Christina would answer with both honesty and comfort: Is my bed gone? Yes, Anna, your bed is gone. Is my quilt gone? Yes, Alina, your quilt is gone. Is Mr. Potato Head gone? Yes, girls, I'm afraid he is.

The schools were, of course, closed, as was almost everything. Darwin tried to distract the children with a deck of cards. He taught the girls how to play fish, war, and snap and, in the evening, they all played cards together, the six of them, by the warm light of the oil lamp. Julie found the girls to be surprisingly respectful of her things and offered them a couple of rudimentary piano lessons and all of her Belgian chocolates. Anna drew a splendid picture of Julie playing the piano, which Julie taped to the wall prominently and proudly. They ate pizza noon and night two days in a row because, well, why not, and there were plenty of uptown businesses making the most of emerging delivery opportunities.

At one point, Julie said something to Darwin that would stay warm in his soul for the rest of his life. She said, "You would have been a good father." And at another point, Darwin said something to Julie that gave her great hope and joy. He said, "Maybe we should consider getting a dog."

When, on the third day following the storm, the lights returned to Midtown Manhattan, the Margas family moved into a hotel, one that would allow them to keep Dragoi with them. The Wilsons orchestrated this arrangement, and both Darwin and Julie were pleased that the family would now have more of the privacy they undoubtedly needed. Disappointed for themselves, however, because they had become unexpectedly attached to this hard-working brave little family who were facing a mountain of change.

Hurricane Sandy brought layers of devastation that continued to be discovered and uncovered in the days ahead. The monster storm brought out the worst in a few miserable and unmentionable people, but it brought out the very best in most. In fact, as Darwin reflected, the storm did, as his father had suggested, summon the very face of God into a morass of loss and fear, the very shining face of God to which the Psalm referred. And Julie and Darwin were happy to be counted among those who, in the sometimes overwhelming darkness and in the face of their own fears, had cast at a little divine light.

Grace to you and peace from God our Father and the Lord Jesus Christ. I give thanks to my God always for you because of the grace of God that has been given you in Christ Jesus, for in every way you have been enriched in him, in speech and knowledge of every kind—just as the testimony of Christ has been strengthened among you—so that you are not lacking in any spiritual gift as you wait for the revealing of our Lord Jesus Christ. He will also strengthen you to the end, so that you may be blameless on the day of our Lord Jesus Christ. God is faithful; by him you were called into the fellowship of his Son, Jesus Christ our Lord.

—1 Corinthians 1:3–9, NRSV, A Reading for the First Sunday of Advent, Year B

5
Ernie & the Thankless Heathens

ERNIE ADAMS HAD LIVED on this earth and in the great State of Maine for eighty-four years. With a sharp mind, a prickly wit, a diploma from the academy, and a degree in education from up to Farmington, he still felt number than a hake most of the time. Thanksgiving had come and gone. Once again, he'd dined with the neighbors. Once more, he brought a pie with him—one of those pies that the teenagers made over to the church for an annual ski-trip fundraiser. He ordered raspberry this year for a change and it tasted pretty dang good. He longingly remembered the warm, sweet pie mounded with velvety vanilla ice cream.

Ernie didn't stick with teaching, although his own mother, God rest her soul, had taught English most of her life. Like a cat that falls overboard and develops an immediate revulsion to swimming, Ernie discovered right quick that he didn't much care for kids who seemed endlessly full of sneezes and fidgets. Ernie realized he shouldn't blame them– they were just being kids—but he had no patience for them, and there was no use pretending he did.

So he spent most of his life doing what he really wanted to do anyway. He went fishing—lobster fishing. Though it was demanding work, he couldn't imagine a better office or a more satisfying way to make a living. As a spry eighty-four year old with a strong back and a stubborn constitution, he still worked a few traps. Besides, there was no one to stop him, no one to tell him it was time to give up this or stop doing that. His wife, Darlene, God bless her, had been in the arms of the Lord for more than twenty years. But he still talked to her. All the time.

His daughter, Christie, was a different matter altogether. Christie had moved to Maryland decades ago, right after marrying. The marriage fell apart after nine years, but Christie remained faithful to Maryland. Christie and the girls, three of them, used to come home to Maine twice a year, once in July and once at Christmas. After Darlene died, however, they stopped coming altogether. No matter how hard he tried, he could not persuade them to visit. Part of it, Ernie knew, was the whole patience bit. Darlene had been an angel with kids, an angel with everyone. Patient and kind, she greased the family wheels effortlessly. Ernie, however, was a bit of a porcupine and he knew that. At the age of eighty-four, his essential personality was not going to change.

Ernie called them all the "thankless heathens." "They're nothing but a bunch of 'thankless heathens,'" he told the spirit of Darlene. He could still hear her voice, Darlene's bright warm voice filled with gentle, humor-filled nudging. "Oh, Ernie," he heard her say. "Oh, Ernie." Neither death nor mounting years could take that beloved voice away from him.

He called them 'thankless' because, every year, he and Darlene had gone out of their way to find out what those girls would like for Christmas. And every year they went out of their way to get whatever those girls claimed they needed—even though, it seemed to Ernie, they never really needed anything. Years upon years of dolls, games, clothes. And not once in all those years did anyone ever send a 'thank you' note. Darlene, of course, instructed them every year not to bother with 'thank you' notes. Ernie, however, felt that was no excuse.

He called them 'heathens' because they never went to church. For all Ernie knew, although they had never discussed it, Christie didn't even believe in God. Ernie knew this had broken Darlene's heart. All those years of teaching Sunday School, all those years of serving on one time-consuming committee after another. She made a huge investment with no return that Ernie could see as he considered Christie's unfamiliar life in far-away Maryland.

Ernie & the Thankless Heathens

When he referred to them as the "thankless heathens," his friend, Rick, reminded him of his own somewhat irregular church attendance. But it was so hard. "Church isn't the same without you, Darlene," he whispered. "Oh, Ernie," came the faithful voice.

Christie would turn 60 next year. She had become the impressive teacher he never could be. Funny how some of these things seem to skip a generation. Christie's girls were grown, city girls—every one of them. Two lived and worked in Washington, D.C., but the middle girl lived closer—Boston. She was a teacher too. The girls called him every couple of weeks or so, but they seemed to have lost their way to Maine. And when Christmas arrived, well, over the years, the carefully chosen gifts turned into gift certificates, then into checks. "That way," suggested Christie, "they can pick out what they really need." Whether gifts or cash, the heathens remain thankless and, as far as Ernie could tell, they still needed nothing. "Oh, Ernie, give 'em a break," came Darlene's voice.

The phone interrupted conflicting feelings of abandonment and hope. "Good mornin', Romeo," said Rick.

"Mornin' to you, Romeo," replied Ernie, "and Happy Thanksgiving."

Rick and Ernie and three other widowers ate out on a regular basis and called themselves the Romeos—r-o-m-e-o, which stands for 'retired old men eating out.'

"You got an extra dining room table out there in your barn, right?"

"Ayuh," replied Ernie with a touch of misgiving.

"I hear tell there's a bunch a them ee-vacu-ees from New Orleans moved up to Portland."

"And?"

"Well you know, they need everything—beds, coats, dining room tables." Rick said that last part real slow so that Ernie wouldn't miss the point.

"So, what's your point?" asked Ernie.

"Put your shoes on, Ernie, the Romeos are renting a big truck and we're gonna fill the dang thing and pretend we're Christians for a day." He added, "And if you have any good old coats, drag those out of storage, too. They need coats."

Ernie went up into the barn and looked at the good walnut table that had been in Darlene's family. "Should I really do this, Darlene?" he asked. "Oh Ernie, don't be numb as a hake," came the adored voice, "Let it go."

By the time Rick pulled up to the back of the barn, Ernie had dragged the table out and gathered up a wheelbarrow full of warm clothing, including his old wool letter jacket from the Academy. Although 65 years old, it looked almost new—clean and wrinkle-free, hanging in a clear garment bag. He'd kept it thinking there might someday be a legacy, a thankless heathen who would end up at his alma mater and might want to have his old well-kept wool jacket. But it was time to put that idea to rest once and for all.

Rick had organized the whole mission project. He had gathered up enough cookware, dishware, silverware, linens, beds, dressers, and dining room sets for every family brave enough to leave the south and face the Maine winter. And those old Romeos, all in their eighties yet strong as bucks, hauled it all down to Portland.

Grateful faces met them, some with teary eyes as they helped unload the furnishings of their new lives in Maine. Ernie couldn't remember witnessing a greater need or a deeper gratitude. Everyone helped carry the second-hand treasures.

The high spot of the day occurred when, out of the corner of his eye, Ernie spied a tall, lanky café-skinned teenager sorting through the pile of coats. Ernie turned for a closer look. Like a magician pulling from the deck the very card the audience has in mind, the boy wrestled his old letter jacket from the huge pile. The boy put it on and hugged himself warm in it. In spite of his loneliness, cantankerousness and frequent number-than-a-hake feeling, this perfectly enriching moment, filled Ernie with a sense of well-being. Darlene was right there with him, saying, "Oh, Ernie, would you look at that!"

After the deliveries were made and the truck was returned, the Romeos went out to the local diner for its famous fried scallop basket special. During dinner, they hatched a plan to surprise the evacuees with Christmas presents. And right there and then, Ernie Adams made a decision, a decision he was sure Darlene would understand.

He would send the girls Christmas cards without checks this year. He would write a note to each of them and explain the whole plan to help these evacuees who had lost nearly everything. And the girls would understand. Even the thankless heathens would understand such a thing. He stared at the beautiful old picture of Darlene that hung above the fireplace and asked, "They will understand, won't they dear?" "Oh, Ernie," she replied deep within his ornery soul, "Of course they will."

Do not ignore this one fact, beloved, that with the Lord one day is like a thousand years, and a thousand years are like one day. The Lord is not slow about his promise, as some think of slowness, but is patient with you, not wanting any to perish, but all to come to repentance. But the day of the Lord will come like a thief, and then the heavens will pass away with a loud noise, and the elements will be dissolved with fire, and the earth and everything that is done on it will be disclosed.

Since all these things are to be dissolved in this way, what sort of persons ought you to be in leading lives of holiness and godliness, waiting for and hastening the coming of the day of God, because of which the heavens will be set ablaze and dissolved, and the elements will melt with fire? But, in accordance with God's promise, we wait for new heavens and a new earth, where righteousness is at home. Therefore, beloved, while you are waiting for these things, strive to be found by God at peace, without spot or blemish.

—2 Peter 3: 8–14, NRSV, A Reading for the Second Sunday of Advent, Year B

6
The Patience of P.J.

P.J. WAS WORRIED ABOUT his Christmas Cactus. Actually, he was driving his parents crazy over the Christmas Cactus but he couldn't help himself. He loved that plant. His Grammy in Nevada had shipped it to him for his birthday. Arriving three weeks early on a big brown truck in a large white box with his name on it, Peter James, and it had to be signed for, and his mother let him sign.

His mom loved to tell the story of how *he* had arrived three weeks early on the very morning when she planned to shop in the annual early bird Christmas shopping extravaganza where, if you dress up in up your pajamas, you receive a big discount. His mother did wear her pajamas that morning but, as she enjoyed telling everyone, instead of getting a discount, she got him. In honor of the occasion, she named him "Peter James," knowing, from that moment on, she would call him P.J., her early bird special.

Last summer on their annual pilgrimage to Nevada, (what Grammy called "Holy Ground" because you could walk around without shoes all year long), P.J. had been quite taken with all of Grammy's plants and especially the one with dazzling cascades of crimson blooms at the tip of every lizard leg of cactus. "That one will grow in Maine," she told P.J. at the time, pointing to the Christmas Cactus. "All these others? Forget it. Too cold. Too damp. Too unpredictable."

"What's un-pruh-dick-able?" P.J. asked his Grammy.

"That's when you never know what the weather's going to do," she answered.

"You mean like rain?" he asked.

"Rain, snow, sleet, hail, fog—you can have it, P.J."

"But I like snow, and I like fog, Grammy."

"That's good," his Grammy said, "you live in the right place."

The Christmas Cactus arrival thrilled P.J. He heard his mother whisper into the phone to his Grammy, "What kind of present is that for a six-year-old boy?" but P.J. thought it was the best present anyone ever gave him. He loved it even more than his Red Sox jersey and he loved that jersey the way a tortoise loves its shell. Just last week, P.J. heard his mother whispering on the phone again, "He's gonna love that foolish plant to death. He waters it twice a day!" His mom kept yelling at him for watering the plant too much. "Peter James," she called (which only happened when matters were quite serious), "you're gonna drown that thing." But, once again, P.J. couldn't help it. He didn't want the plant to be thirsty. He didn't want it to be hungry either so, when his mom wasn't looking, he had poked some raisins into the soil and buried a Hershey's kiss in there and then, assuming that what was good for growing children had to be good for growing plants, he poured a little apple juice on the already moist soil.

One by one, the tiny buds had fallen off their rigid spikey legs and then the legs got soft like overcooked pasta and the whole plant seemed to collapse. His mom told him she was going to have to take the plant to the plant hospital, where they could make it healthy again. "Where's the plant hospital?" P.J. wanted to know. "It's on the way to the people hospital," his mom assured him but he couldn't remember ever seeing a plant hospital before. In the very same conversation, P.J.s older sister, Delilah, told him that the plant hospital was actually on the way to the compost pile. "Don't be cruel, Delilah Jean," their mother said in a voice that was unmistakably exasperated. P.J.'s sister's name was Delilah but everybody called her "Dilly" and P.J. called her "Dilly Bean" because he liked Dilly Beans and he liked his big sister—most of the time. Although she didn't always seem to like him.

Dilly was fourteen—eight years older than P.J. Sometimes she treated him as she would a pest, swatting the air when she wanted him to go away. "There is no plant hospital," he heard his sister whisper to their mom. P.J. couldn't understand what all the whispering was about when everybody perfectly well that hearing was one of his superpowers. Hearing and staying awake late, staying up well beyond the capacity of most six-year-olds, were P.J.'s two best superpowers.

Apparently failing to remember these powers, his mother whispered back to Dilly, "Do you want to break your little brother's heart? The plant hospital is called "The Greenhouse & Garden Shop."

"Well, I hope there's a plant heaven next to the plant hospital," Dilly murmured.

"Shhh," his mom said, staring at Dilly as if she had horns.

"Unless they're selling miracles at the Greenhouse, that plant is heading for Christmas Cactus heaven, Mom, and you know it. I think I saw him put one of his Superman vitamins in that pot."

"Did not!" P.J. piped up.

"Did too!" Dilly retorted.

"Did not!"

"Did too!"

"Be kind," their mom chided. Then she walked over to P.J., put warm protective arms all the way around him and announced, "It's going to be fine." P.J. believed his mother absolutely.

The next day, the Christmas cactus disappeared and his mom told him she had taken it to the plant hospital. He trusted her because she was his mom, but he continued to worry. In fact, he worried so well he was beginning to wonder if that might be another of his peculiar superpowers. That night, as his dad tucked him in, and as he worried once more about the limp plant, he asked, "You sure my Christmas Cactus didn't get stoled?"

"Stolen," he corrected, "no, it didn't get stolen."

"A lot of stuff has been stoled around here," he reminded his dad.

"Yes, a lot of stuff has been *stolen* around here lately," he repeated.

And that was sadly true. In a year when folks were losing jobs and having trouble paying bills and buying groceries, a disturbing number of thefts had occurred—even from places like the library and the church. P.J.'s own father was without work and, as you can well imagine, there was a lot of whispering in the house about that. His mother assured P.J. often, however, that his father *would* find a job and someday his sister *would* be nicer to him and the plant hospital *would* fix his plant in time for Christmas. "We just need patience," she announced. "And prayer," she added in a whisper.

P.J. knew all about prayer. He learned in Sunday School how you could tell God just about anything and ask God for just about anything as long as it wasn't something you really didn't need like an X-box or a Chunky Monkey Sundae. Every night, P.J. prayed for his Dad to find a job and for his mom not to be so troubled and for his plant to get better and grow flowers. But he wasn't exactly sure what patience was so he waited and asked his father the next day when he came home from job searching. "Patience. Good question, P.J.," his father affirmed. Nobody made P.J. feel as good about himself as his Dad. "Patience is waiting for something to happen when waiting is hard."

"But I'm tired of waiting."

"Well, patience, P.J., is *not* getting tired of waiting."

"How do you do that, Dad?"

"Well, one thing you have to remember, P.J., is that God's time is not like our time. A whole year is like a minute to God and a whole month is like a second."

"That's really weird, Dad," P.J. responded, trying to wrap his young mind around the supple nature of time and the tough challenge of patience.

"Dad, I have another question.

"Go on."

"Do they sell miracles at the plant hospital?"

"Where?"

"The plant hospital."

"The plant hospital?"

"The plant hospital at the Greenhouse."

"Oh, the *Greenhouse*."

"Mom says they sell miracles there."

"Mom ought to know," is all his father had to say about that.

"Can God go back in time?" P.J. continued his query.

"I suppose."

"Can God go forward in time?"

"I suppose."

"I wish I could go forward in time."

"Why's that?" his dad asked.

"Then my plant would be all better, and I could see it again."

"Well, you can do that," his dad suggested, "in that precocious head of yours." P.J. had heard the word precocious before. It was like another superpower. "You can use your imagination, P.J. Just imagine that Christmas Cactus back on the kitchen counter feeling better and looking great all loaded with flowers."

"I like that," said P.J., "I can see it in my head."

The weeks passed slowly. P.J. wondered what those plodding weeks were like for God. Maybe they were like something even smaller than a second. And then, all of a sudden, after all that measured waiting, Christmas Eve arrived. P.J. had done a pretty good job of not mentioning his plant too much, mostly because he didn't want to hear his mom say, "You're driving us crazy," one more time and he didn't want to see her "that's enough, P.J." look anymore.

Christmas Eve is, of course, the perfect time to use the "staying awake" superpower. That night, after church and after dinner and after his bath and after he was tucked in, P.J. put that power to good use, along with his super-hearing. He knew this Christmas would be smaller because his dad still didn't have a job but all P.J. really wanted was to have his Christmas Cactus back and to see it bloom. And maybe a spiraling foam football or a radio-controlled gyro-bot or Spiderman underpants.

Pondering the possibilities while visions of cactus blooms danced in his precocious little head, suddenly he heard his mom say, "I thought you were going to pick up the plant." "No, you said you were going to get it," his dad replied. And P.J. had a sinking feeling in his belly. He wasn't so excited about Christmas anymore and he wished he didn't have any superpowers. He put his whole head under the covers and prayed, "Dear God, let me fall asleep." Then he curled up tight, put his hands over his ears, and fell into the darkness where time has no influence and patience is unnecessary and all things are possible.

On Christmas morning, P.J. took his time coming down into the kitchen. His parents, already awake, sipped black coffee and nibbled on a sweet coffee cake that his Sunday School teacher had dropped off. Dilly Bean was probably still in bed. Sleeping late was one of her super-powers. "Merry Christmas," his mom said cheerfully. "Merry Christmas," he responded cautiously. He went over to his parents and received a hug from each of them. Summoning all available hope and all accessible imagination, he looked to the place on the kitchen counter where his cactus used to sit. It was not there. He poked his head around the corner into the living room and surveyed the small pile of gifts beneath the tree. No Christmas cactus. As he shook his head in disappointment, determined not to cry, down low in the corner of his eye, he spied a full head of bright red flowers. His Christmas cactus sat smack in the middle of the fireplace like a burning bush where there was no fire. It looked smaller but he figured a sick plant might shrink a little. It was in a different pot but the doctors at the plant hospital probably had to do that.

"They fixed it! They fixed it!" he cried.

"What are you talking about?" his father asked and both parents rounded the corner to witness the little miracle. They stared at each other in amazement. "I didn't do it," his mother whispered to his father, as if P.J. couldn't hear. "It wasn't me," his father whispered back.

P.J. was hugging the blooming plant in such a way that his chin appeared to have sprouted a cactus beard. Dilly Bean padded into the living room. She came up behind her astonished parents, stretched her arms around their shoulders and, beaming with satisfaction, she whispered, "I have a few superpowers too, you know."

It was a year steeped in tough times. It was a year of praying for the stock market and the job market. It was a year of figuring out that there is such a thing as too little income and too much worry and too much water! It was a year for remembering that God's time is not our time. It was a year for learning the importance of kindness and the power of patience.

When the Lord restored the fortunes of Zion, we were like those who dream.

Then our mouth was filled with laughter, and our tongue with shouts of joy;

then it was said among the nations, "The Lord has done great things for them."

The Lord has done great things for us, and we rejoiced.

Restore our fortunes, O Lord, like the watercourses in the Negeb.

May those who sow in tears reap with shouts of joy.

Those who go out weeping, bearing the seed for sowing, shall come home with shouts of joy, carrying their sheaves.

—Psalm 126, NRSV, A Reading for the Third Sunday of Advent, Year B

Rejoice always, pray without ceasing, give thanks in all circumstances; for this is the will of God in Christ Jesus for you. Do not quench the Spirit. Do not despise the words of prophets, but test everything; hold fast to what is good; abstain from every form of evil. May the God of peace sanctify you entirely; and may your spirit and soul and body be kept sound and blameless at the coming of our Lord Jesus Christ. The one who calls you is faithful, and will do this.

—1 Thessalonians 5:16–24, NRSV, A Reading for the Third Sunday of Advent, Year B

7
Aught of Joy

TALYA KAYA WAS DREADFULLY homesick. With every ounce of her stubbornly independent being, Talya had dreamed, longed, ached to leave her home in Turkey and to procure a first-class college education in the United States. She also wanted to experience American culture, to absorb the glamour, energy and creativity she associated with America. The first few weeks were truly glorious as she became acquainted with her two fantastic American roommates and ate hamburgers and fries and watched perhaps too much American television.

Now, however, after almost four months, she yearned to be home again with her mother and father and three bubbly younger sisters. She longed to sit around the dinner table in her own home with her own family. She imagined sharing the stories she'd gathered over the last few exhilarating months and listening to their stories. She could almost taste her mother's delicious köfte—savory Turkish meatballs.

At the age of nineteen, Talya, the eldest of the four daughters in the Kaya family, was destined, therefore, to be the most serious, the most responsible. This was, in no small measure, because so much was expected of her. Her parents, especially her father, held high hopes for her. "Talya will be the first woman President of Turkey!" her father boasted to his friends, "She is smart like Orhan Pamuk" *(the famous Turkish author)*; "she is strong like Nurcan Taylan" *(the petite female Turkish weightlifter)*.

While Talya appreciated her father's pride, her stomach turned uneasily when he spoke like that. She did not wish to be a writer. Her goal was to become a sociologist. And she was too skinny and far too busy reading to spend her time lifting weights. Furthermore, she knew her shyness would not suit a political career.

Talya had worked diligently to gain acceptance at the prestigious Bowdoin College in picturesque Maine. Her parents and grandfather, who supported their enlightened and independent child, worked very hard to pay her tuition and keep her there. Right now, nevertheless, visions of home overwhelmed her: visions of her own soft bed and her own downy pillow and her own comfortable family. Talya could not afford to go home, however, until the end of May. She hoped hoped hoped she would not feel this empty, this homesick, for five more months.

As her classmates departed for home for Christmas break, Talya's nostalgia for home was swollen by the fact that almost all of the other freshman students had gone home for Christmas break. They had chatted at length about their families, their homes, their mothers' Christmas cookies. Then, like a flock of birds that sit up on a wire for hours but suddenly departs in a flurry, the American students had left and they had left her behind. One of her roommates, Katie, dear Katie, had invited Talya to go home with her to South Carolina but Talya had gratefully declined. While she would never let on to her roommates, she could not possibly afford a round-trip plane ticket to South Carolina. And so, Talya would be mostly alone for the next four weeks. Putting the best possible face of it, this break would give her time to catch up, time to study, and time in one of her favorite places in the world, the library.

The Bowdoin library would remain open during much of the Christmas break, but the dormitories would be closed for nearly a month. Talya felt fortunate to be staying, for the duration of the break, in a very nice apartment temporarily vacated by four seniors. Her job was to look after their cat, an enormous white beast named "P. Bear", and to keep the place relatively neat and tidy. In kind return, the renters were not charging her anything to stay in their apartment.

Talya was not a huge fan of cats but so far, she and P. Bear were getting along better than anticipated. He rubbed up against her legs affectionately when she came in from the library. He purred gratefully when she fed him a can of strong smelling feline food. Why Bear even jumped up onto the end of her bed at night as if to keep her December feet warm! Perhaps Talya had never given cats a fair chance simply because her family had never owned one. Cats were, in fact, highly revered in Turkey. Islamic lore told of a cat who redirected a dangerous snake so that it would not reach the Prophet Muhammad.

Talya was fairly certain she did not believe such myths but P. Bear offered her good company on this lonely Christmas break. Oh, she had more substantial offers of company. Bowdoin had a host family program through which local families took international students under their wings. Talya's host family was very nice, a family of six with four daughters—like her own family. But these girls were all little—ages two, four, seven, and nine—all with saffron hair and morning glory eyes. The four-year-old, named Sophie, reminded her of her own littlest sister, Damla, now fourteen-years-old. Both girls were fearless, funny, and shameless flirts.

Damla often poked fun at her big sister, Talya, calling her Ciddi[1]. You should have been named, "Ciddi," Damla teased. Ciddi means: boring, dull, starched, no fun. Talya poked back, saying, "Well, you're too much fun!" It was true that Talya led a fairly serious life. She didn't smile much. She tried. She wanted to be fun, to find and feel joy, but there was work to be done; books to digest, tests to conquer and thoughts to absorb. After all, that's why she came to this fairly remote New England town.

As her lonely December days proceeded, Talya's host family called several times to check on her and to invite her to this dinner or that party. Despite their relentless hospitality, Talya politely declined each time. Nevertheless, when Tina Ashford called her a few days before, she told her that the girls were begging to see her and had made her something for Christmas. Wouldn't she consider coming for dinner on Christmas Eve?" Talya relented. They

---

1. Pronounced: Jĭddy.

also invited her to their church for the Christmas Eve candlelight service but Talya felt uncomfortable about that piece of the invitation. She would come for dinner but skip the church service.

She had been inside many churches, some of them beautiful ancient churches in Turkey, but she had never attended a Christian worship service. Talya's family, nominally Muslim, did not practice their faith. As a little girl, she occasionally went to a special holiday celebration in her neighborhood mosque, but that was the extent of her religious upbringing. Talya believed in a Deity, in a creator of the universe called by many names, here—God, there—Allah. She supposed that this Deity must have spoken through Mohammed, although it seemed that human beings sometimes put self-serving words in his mouth. She supposed that this same Deity must have spoken through Jesus, although as far as she could tell, people put some strange words in his mouth too.

The idea that any religion would claim to be the only way to access God troubled Talya, yet all seemed to do this very thing in one way or another. In any event, while she could see the academic benefit of observing a Christian worship service, she felt uncomfortable doing so. Perhaps at some future point but not yet. And so Talya determined to go to the Ashford home for Christmas Eve dinner but not accompany them to church.

Late on the afternoon of Christmas Eve, Talya walked downtown to the quaint floral shop in Brunswick and bought a bouquet of crimson tulips. They not only seemed the right color for a Christmas house but they were, also indirectly, a gift from Turkey. Most of the world thought of Holland when they saw tulips, but the Dutch originally imported these beautiful flowers from Turkey. The tulips were not inexpensive but Talya wanted to bring the Ashfords a special gift, a suitable gift. She also searched for a small gift for the girls in a small but well-stocked candy shop a few doors down from the florist. The fragrance of chocolate and traditional sweets of the season filled the air. She bought four small but impressive hand-made candy canes, each beribboned in green satin.

The Ashfords lived near the Bowdoin campus and she took her time walking from the downtown area of Brunswick to their stately home, carefully carrying her well-wrapped gifts, passing an array of light displays on almost every house. This tradition was all new to Talya. She had seen light displays before but never anything like this. Americans, she noticed, were generally happy people but they were especially elated during this season of lights and decorations and parties and presents. Their special word for happy at this time of year—jolly-was new to her. Jolly. She liked it. Talya's English was quite good and she loved adding new words to her vocabulary.

Like so many of their neighbors, the Ashfords decorated with outdoor lights, theirs complete with what she thought must be reindeer (although they could have been moose—she wasn't sure). As she approached their front door, she could see a tall evergreen tree inside the house, laden with colored lights and shiny ornaments. In every window, a soft white candle flickered. Talya was suddenly very glad she had accepted the Ashfords' invitation, not only from a sociological point of view but because, eventually, she would share this experience with her little sister, Damla. Damla would get to hear, first-hand, how much fun her big sister was having in America.

She let the big brass knocker shaped as a radiant sun fall gently three times. Tina met her at the door surrounded by four very excited little girls who were jumping and shrieking, "Yay! She's here! She's here!" Little Sophie yelled, "We made somefing for you!" clearly pleased that she was the first of the sisters to announce this good news. The girls were dressed all alike in dark green velvet dresses with silky white collars and little bright red berries embroidered on the bodice of each. They wore shiny black patent leather shoes over red and white candy cane tights, the sight of which prompted Talya to think of the sticky gifts she had brought for them. Tom Ashford came out from the kitchen wearing a Santa-belted apron, his hands damp from kitchen chores.

They took her coat and hat and gloves and seemed delighted by the stunning red tulips, which Tina quickly arranged in a tall crystal vase. Tina and Tom had outdone themselves. They had stealthily gathered information on Talya's favorite Turkish dishes, preparing Turkish meatballs, rice with cardamom, eggplant, fresh bread, and for dessert, almond cookies with something approximating Turkish coffee. How had they known? Talya wondered. How had they known how much she was missing the tastes of home?

Deeply touched by the extravagant hospitality of the Ashford family, she was nearly overcome with rare emotion by what happened next. After dinner, while Tom and Tina cleaned up, refusing any of Talya's pleas to help, the girls dragged her into the living room with great energy and sat her in a chair next to their bejeweled aromatic balsam. "Close your eyes," they said. "Yeah, c'ose 'em," said Sophie who was still struggling with diphthongs. Talya complied, a small smile escaping her lips as she felt a big box land in her lap.

"Open your eyes!" they shouted. When she did, she saw an obviously kid-wrapped gift box covered in wrinkled white tissue paper with a glittery red bow affixed to the top by at least four layers of cellophane tape. "Open it! Open it!" they shrieked, unable to contain their excitement. By now Talya was beaming. She couldn't help it. She tore into the white tissue and opened the box. Inside was a little Christmas tree covered with tiny ornaments which the girls had fashioned out of painted macaroni, colorful plastic buttons, miniature marshmallows fashioned into snowmen, and baby angels formed of lace. "Doos you like it?" Sophie asked.

"Do I like it? I love it," responded Talya, her face aglow with joy. I'm going to take it back to the apartment and put it right next to my bed. The girls seemed very satisfied with her answer. "And I have something for you!" Talya announced. "Wait here." She retrieved the little bag she'd left in her coat pocket and gave each of the girls one of the candy canes. It was a small gift compared to theirs but the sheer delight of the Ashford girls could not have been improved upon if she had given them diamond jewelry. Talya was so glad she had come here instead of spending another quiet evening with P. Bear.

Tina poked her pretty head around the corner into the living room and asked brightly, "Are you sure you don't want to come to church with us? It lasts only about an hour and it's so pretty with all the candles." "Please, please, please," the girls begged with Sophie layering a high-pitched "Peas! Peas!" on top of the others. "Girls,

girls, you're not even going to church tonight," their Mom told the girls, "it's bedtime for you."

"No bed!" insisted a disappointed Sophie but the others started whispering "Santa" to her, and her frowning resistance disappeared. Talya said "Goodnight" to each of the girls and waited as Tom and Tina readied them for bed and tucked them in. As Talya waited, she heard the doorbell chime and Tom called down to ask if Talya would answer the door. "It's the babysitter," he added.

The Ashfords dropped Talya off on their way to the 11:00 candlelight service and as she left, Talya thanked them again for the amazing Turkish meal and the wonderful little tree. They asked one last time if she would like to come with them but she answered quietly, "I think I should head back and check on P. Bear."

And so Talya left, filled with the good will that grows in the rich soil of hospitality. She prepared to spend the rest of the evening with P. Bear and chapter six of her Sociology 101 textbook. She found it nearly impossible, though, to open the book and thought again of the Ashford's invitation. If she hurried, she might get to their church before the service started. As P. Bear looked on, ears pinned back in surprise, Talya readied herself to leave again, gave the kitty a quick scratch on the head, and assured him that she would be home soon.

Talya raced down the sidewalk along the Maine Street side of campus, not stopping to catch her breath until she neared the tall main doors of the iconic church. Stepping inside, she was greeted and welcomed and very surprised to find the church completely full—standing room only. The congregation was already singing an opening hymn, a tune Talya had heard before, *O Come, All Ye Faithful, Joyful and Triumphant*. What a joyful sound the congregation made accompanied by an organ so commanding, the sound of it reverberated through the floorboards. Whatever else Christianity was, it was a happy religion, Talya thought.

She was packed into the back of the sanctuary with dozens of other late-comers for whom there were no more seats. Just as she was thinking it was pointless to try to find the Ashfords in such an assembly, the singing crowd parted and made a path through which Tom Ashford moved effortlessly, motioning her to follow. How had he spotted her, Talya wondered, in such a mob as this? She followed him up the center aisle of the church to a pew very near the front.

The pews were also packed but everyone standing in the same row as the Ashfords shifted over, cozying up to one another all the more, and making room for her in the middle, where Tina was simultaneously singing the hymn and nodding to her. Talya thought these people should probably be annoyed at the prospect of adding one more person to an already well-filled pew but, as she squeezed by each person, she heard the word, "Welcome." Three times she heard the word, "welcome" over the exultant sound of the music.

There was a palpable warmth among these people and an audible joy. In her part of the world, Christians were sometimes viewed as scary crusaders with an historic record of destruction and bloodshed. She understood, also, that in this part of the world, Muslims had a similar reputation. But as she sat with Tina and Tom Ashford, listening to the lessons and singing their attendant carols, she heard something altogether different. She heard the prophetic call to peace and the angelic call to joy. In fact, joy seemed to be the recurrent theme of the evening. It was a word that echoed through the service.

One lesson spoke of a harvest of joy. Another preached of rejoicing always. A gospel angel spoke to the terrified shepherds in the fields surrounding Bethlehem, saying, "I bring you good tidings of great joy, which will be for all people." The evening message seemed also to be about the joy to which God calls us. No wonder these Christians were so happy. It was a primary message of their faith. And, in one of those light bulb "I get it" moments, it occurred to Talya that the violent Muslims and the violent Christians had one thing in common—they got the whole thing wrong. They were missing the joy of faith.

Talya rather liked the idea of a vulnerable little baby being in charge of the world rather than the often weapons-obsessed leaders currently ruling the planet. She pondered this bit of sacred genius, this notion of a divine savior wrapped in ordinary human skin. When the Christmas Eve message had ended, the congregation stood to sing a hymn that was unfamiliar to her:

"Watchman, Tell us of the night, what its signs of promise are. Traveler, o'er yon mountain's height, see that glory-beaming star. Watchman, does its beauteous ray aught of joy or hope foretell?"

She stopped. Another new word: Aught. What in the world did "aught" mean? When the congregation sat down, she took a stubby little yellow pencil from a pew rack in front of her and wrote the word: a-u-g-h-t on her paper program.

The final scripture lesson of the evening contained a mysterious message from a book called, *The Gospel According to John*. The worship service ended at midnight with a sharing of soft candlelight that illuminated every face in the sanctuary. A vibrant singing of *Joy to the World* followed, a hymn that fit with her growing understanding of Christmas and Christians.

Before leaving the pew, she asked the Ashfords if she might borrow one of the pew Bibles. Tom personally pulled one of the bright red books out of the pew rack for her, saying, "I'm sure it's fine—just bring it back when you're finished." She tucked the Christmas Eve program into the Bible and, once again, thanked the Ashfords for their many kindnesses.

Back in the apartment with a snuggly P. Bear, Talya looked up the word, "aught" and found that it meant "anything." "Aught of joy," therefore, probably meant "anything of joy" or even "nothing but joy." Perhaps she could get used to this religion, a faith that found joy in a lowly manger, a faith that celebrated joy in the midst of conflict and sang of joy in the face of trouble.

Tucked into her borrowed bed, she found the Gospel of John in the borrowed Bible, and read once more of the Savior born into a borrowed manger. There she read the words she had heard near the end of the service: "In the beginning was the Word and the Word was with God and the word was God." And she whispered to P. Bear, "And the word was joy—aught of joy."

I will sing of the Lord's loyal love forever.

I will proclaim your faithfulness with my own mouth from one generation to the next.

That's why I say, "Your loyal love is rightly built—forever!

You establish your faithfulness in heaven."

You said, "I made a covenant with my chosen one;

I promised my servant David: I will establish your offspring forever;

I will build up your throne from one generation to the next."

—Psalm 89:1–4, CEB, A Reading for the Fourth Sunday of Advent, Year B

May the glory be to God who can strengthen you with my good news and the message that I preach about Jesus Christ. He can strengthen you with the announcement of the secret that was kept quiet for a long time. Now that secret is revealed through what the prophets wrote. It is made known to the Gentiles in order to lead to their faithful obedience based on the command of the eternal God. May the glory be to God, who alone is wise! May the glory be to him through Jesus Christ forever! Amen.

—Romans 16:25–27, CEB, A Reading for the Fourth Sunday of Advent, Year B

8

Not Another Race of Creatures Bound on Other Journeys

BOB WAS EAGER TO get home. He used to enjoy the traveling that goes hand in hand with a career in sales but, at this point in his life, he'd grown weary of the lines, the security, even the meals out because they tended to be so rich. On this trip, he'd been to Denver, Austin, Chicago, Atlanta, and New York, in that order. Now it was time to get back to Bean-town and on home. A blizzard, however, presently blanketed a wide swath of states, grounding planes from Chicago to Boston. Hours before, seasoned travelers, like himself, had secured hotel rooms in which to hunker down until tomorrow or whenever this massive blizzard made its way out to sea. But Bob, well Bob had promised himself and, more importantly, had promised his niece that he would be home tonight. He was hoping, therefore, that a miraculous window would open in this inconvenient storm. If he could get out by late afternoon, he would be home in time for his niece's Christmas Concert or Holiday Jingle Concert or Seasonal Cheer Concert or whatever the heck it was called now.

Bob did not have children of his own but his brother's daughter, Maddie, delighted him. She was so much fun. She loved to play board games and watch good kid movies and bake cookies, and she was always eager to include her beloved Uncle Bob. Bob could not imagine a more gifted little girl than Maddie. If he'd had a child, he would have wanted a daughter just like Maddie—smart, creative, endlessly funny. She would be vocally disappointed if he did not make it to her concert this evening.

Now, Bob generally kept to himself when travelling He worked well with people, a critical job requirement, but he was essentially an introvert. He much preferred a conversation in the comfort of his own head than one with anyone else. The ferocity of the storm, however, kept drawing his gaze to the windows. Each time he looked up, he noticed that some of the less experienced travelers at the gate seemed a little panicky. A small older woman, frail in appearance, sobbed and repeated the same phrase over and over again, "What are we going to do? What are we going to do? What are we going to do? I have to get to my brother's funeral," as her husband shook his head and tried to calm his inconsolable wife. A young smartly dressed professional who had been reading intently propped his chin with one hand, elbows dug into his knees as stared at the blinding snow. He looked a bit like Rodin's thinker dressed in a hip business suit. A young couple with a tiny baby bundled in pink looked pitiably exhausted. An even younger woman, maybe a college student, dressed in form-fitting yoga pants, screamed at the airline check-in agent that this delay was the airline's problem and he had better do something about it. The attendant, with well-practiced forbearance, said, "Sorry, Ma'am, but we have no control over the weather." He was wearing an elf hat with five or six points heading in different directions from the top of his head. "Don't you call me, Ma'am," she responded. "Sorry, Ma'am," the elfin agent retorted with a skillful smile.

The whole world knew this storm was coming but everyone who had journeyed to the airport had, apparently, hoped to beat it or circumnavigate it or wish it away. When most of these would-be passengers had left for the airport, it was snowing steadily but calmly. The airlines were flying planes out as quickly as they could turn them around in advance of what they knew was coming. Now the snow storm had arrived full-force with battalions of small but mighty flakes blowing in an inch an hour. High winds had reduced visibility to near zero. It was time, Bob knew, to get out of that airport one way or another.

However, as he sat there using his smart phone to consider his limited options (rent a car, take a train, spend the night if necessary), something unexpected took hold of Bob. A sudden fire burned in his belly to make things right for the pitiful stragglers who remained with him at the gate. Perhaps it was the time of year, a season of more intentional tenderness. Maybe he felt a bond with these other souls who simply wanted to get where they needed to be. Whatever the reason and whatever the force that was at work within him, Bob quietly and determinedly arose from his choice place in the waiting area, a seat with outlets right behind it (the better to charge one's electronics), walked over to the check-in desk, and politely excused his way between the angry yoga-girl and the patient elf.

"Excuse me just a minute, would you?" Bob interrupted smooth as butter with a smile like sunshine, and what could the young woman do but yield. "May I talk with you privately for just a moment?" Bob gently posed the question and as if in response to Yoda, the Jedi warrior who with a firm but gentle wave of a hand could make people do whatever he wanted, the tall slim elf walked over to one side of the desk with Bob.

"How may I help you?" asked the agent, clearly glad for the reprieve from flummoxed yoga girl.

"Rough day out there," Bob started and the agent nodded swiftly in agreement. "I fly with you a great deal. I love your airline because I know first-hand how you do everything in your power to be helpful to your customers. I've been stuck before, and it seems clear that this plane is not going anywhere today."

"But," interrupted the agent pleasantly, "but we cannot say for certain."

"We both know . . ." Bob said in low thoughtful tones as he nodded in the direction of the television that conveniently displayed a weather map white with heavy snow from Madison to Montpelier, from Indianapolis to Ottawa, "we both know that, barring a miracle, it's over for today." The agent nodded reluctantly.

"So why keep us all here hour after hour when we could be making other plans?"

"You are free, sir, to make other plans. But if you aren't here when the plane departs, I'm afraid I can't help you."

"Yes, but as we know, no plane is taking off or landing in these conditions." Bob motioned to the large plate glass windows on either side of the gate that were being pounded with swarming powder. Bob continued, "I've been eavesdropping on some of your other customers. An elderly couple is trying to get to a family funeral. There is this little baby." Bob made a gratuitously sad face at the thought of this little baby and her parents stuck in a snowy airport. "And, you see, I have a concert to get to. My question is this: If you had to get to Boston today, what would you do?"

Without any hesitation, the agent said, "I'd get to the train station and take the next Amtrak heading north. They keep those tracks clear."

"Can you help us with that please?" The agent offered no visible reaction—no word, no facial expression, no nothing. Bob had already decided that the train provided his best option, and he could simply have left the airport, quietly managing his own transportation. But this room full of stragglers had somehow captured him, and he felt an unexpected responsibility for them.

"Can you get vouchers for all of us who are still here?" Bob continued in spite of the stone-faced answer he had received. "We'll need vouchers for cabs to the station and vouchers for the train from Penn to South Station. I know you can do this."

Still no decipherable response. The agent just stared at him for a very full minute during which time Bob stared back amiably but resolutely. At last, the agent ended the silent show-down, grabbing the phone from his belt and getting to work. There was obviously resistance on the other end of the line. Bob could almost hear the questions being directed at the elf: What do they want? Are you kidding me? How many? "Looks like about a dozen," the agent said as he looked around the gate and counted with his index finger. After another awkwardly long period of time, the airline agent called Bob over and with the shrug of the shoulders said, "I tried."

"You tried and . . ."

"I tried and we'll see. We're not saying 'no' but we're not saying 'yes.'"

"Thank you, I'll wait," Bob said and then got on his own phone with his boss who got on the phone with her superior who got on the phone with some upper echelon airline type. Lo and behold, the agent at the desk with the green and red hat, who had been seen counting the waiting customers again, in short order, came up with 14 cab vouchers, 14 train vouchers, and, miracle of miracles, 14 snack vouchers for airport concessions.

Now, this was all new territory to Bob, who gathered up the little band of passengers and found himself unfolding the plan before them. They were aiming for a three o'clock train, very doable even with snowy city streets. Bob had the group get in line for their vouchers, invited them to grab a snack for the road if they could do it in a timely fashion, and told them he would meet them at the taxi stand—"Just downstairs and outside." The older couple looked confused and Bob added, "Just get your vouchers and follow me. We'll get you to Boston." The couple looked a little dazed but they gathered up their coats and several large shopping bags and followed Bob. All 14 passengers fell in line without delay, some of them obviously quite desperate to be liberated from the increasingly socked-in airport, others clearly delighted that a path through the storm had been found for them. Not surprisingly, the irritated young woman was first in line. Bob made himself last.

I must tell you, Bob was not a get-at-the-end-of-the-line sort of guy. He was not a warm fuzzy love-your-neighbor type. He was not much of leader either really. He was a reasonably successful 42-year-old software salesman who kept to himself much of the time. Today, however, he became someone he had never met before, and no one was more astounded by his actions than he. A plump middle-aged woman, vouchers in hand, said to him, "You are a Godsend." She seemed to be covered in bells—bells on her hat, bells in her earrings, little red and gold bells around her neck. He shook his head in humble disagreement but she continued to nod nevertheless, producing affirming jingles.

As Bob looked out at the blustering snow, he thought that his niece's concert might well be cancelled tonight. And with that thought, the urgency of the day was released from him like air from a full balloon. His niece couldn't possibly be disappointed if he didn't show up for a cancelled concert. A cancelled concert could change everything. He could find a room somewhere, take himself out for a scotch and a nice hot dinner, maybe even find an old Christmas movie on television. The more he thought about this tempting possibility, the more certain he became that they would reschedule Maddie's concert on a night such as this.

With this realization, Bob could have blown off his fellow passengers and headed for a Marriott. But, once again, he found himself strangely committed to this baker's dozen of fellow passengers who for various reasons needed to get to Boston or beyond. And so, with that same energizing fire in his belly that seemed to take hold of him out of nowhere, he collected his own vouchers, at which point the airline agent removed his elf hat and ceremoniously placed it on Bob's head. It was unlike Bob to wear anything that might draw attention to himself but he smiled and left it on. Why not? He would never see any of these people again after today.

On his way out, the newly crowned head elf grabbed a cruller and a cup of Joe to go. With the anxious older couple stuck to him like glue, he met the other frustrated travelers at the taxi queue. The pushy yoga girl had taken off already but the others were standing in the cold, eagerly awaiting their newfound leader. Bob filled each cab and instructed the drivers to take their charges to the 7th Avenue entrance to Penn Station. He was the last of the bunch to get into a taxi, along with the hip young man he'd witnessed holding his chin in his hand. He was a good looking young fellow who, like so many other young men these days, looked as if he'd taken his wardrobe right out of the early 1960s—pencil thin trousers with tailored jacket, thickly rimmed black glasses, clean-shaven, short carefully combed hair. Bob looked down at his own somewhat baggy trousers and promised himself a few personal wardrobe updates.

"Thanks," the dapper young man said once they were on their way. "No problem," Bob said, "We'll get to Boston come hell or high water."

"Not sure about the hell or high water. Come hail or high wind is more like it."

Bob laughed and assured his fellow traveler that, "The trains are pretty good when it comes to snow. We might be late but we will get there. By the way, I'm Bob."

"Nice to meet you, Bob, I'm Eric."

Bob learned that Eric was heading to Boston to spend a holiday weekend with his girlfriend. In fact, he would be meeting her family for the first time and was a little nervous about it. They'd originally met online and then visited one another in their respective cities, New York and Boston. "We hit it off immediately," Eric announced, adding, "I think she's the one."

When they arrived at Penn Station, the others were waiting for him and followed the cheerfully capped Bob through what was a familiar way station for him in his many travels. At the ticket window, he explained to the Amtrak representative what was happening. "You're not the first vouchers today," she said, pointing to crowded waiting areas. Bob noticed yoga girl pacing the hall as she chatted on her cell phone. He then bravely asked if the vouchers might be good for business class and the representative answered with a wink, "I think we can do that." Vouchers were exchanged for tickets, and the wandering crowd located a plush business class car with a snack bar.

Yoga-girl ended up in coach and was furious when she discovered the upgrade the others had landed. She entered their car and started giving the engineer a mouthful of indignation. Bob shook his head in bewildered silence. He thought about advocating on her behalf but dismissed the idea until . . . well, until she started to cry. All of the bluster disappeared from her demeanor as she told the conductor that this was the worst day of her life. She wasn't supposed to be going home until next week when her Christmas break from college started. But her frighteningly ill mother had taken a turn for the worse and was now in intensive care. In a whimper, she said, "I just want to see her. I have to see her. And this storm—this blizzard—it's all a mess."

Bob relented, got up out of his comfortable seat, walked over to the young woman and explained to the conductor that she was with them. She was with the group from the airport and somehow had become separated from the rest. "Sorry, sir, you'll have to go back to the ticket counter and discuss it there. Quite frankly, sir, there's not much time."

"Then, she can have my seat," Bob offered. The source of all this unforeseen altruism was a mystery to Bob. He seemed to have tapped into a fresh and unfamiliar well of big-heartedness.

"Or," said the conductor, "I can upgrade her ticket for thirty-seven dollars." And just like that, possessed of a strength and a spirit he did not understand and could not resist, he took out his wallet and counted out thirty-seven dollars. Yoga-girl, her eyes red and dewy with tears, appeared confused and said nothing.

The others watched the whole transaction and, as Bob headed back to his seat, one of them tugged at his coat sleeve, exclaiming, "You're an angel." The woman with all the bells said, "You're our shepherd today," and the man sitting next to her said, "He's like Moses!" Bob shook his head uncomfortably as he struggled to remember who Moses was (the dude with the ark? the dude with the whale?). Bell-woman, discerning his apparent bewilderment, added, "You know, 'Let my people go,' Red Sea, promised land, Ten Commandments?" Bob had never mastered any of those biblical names. He'd been to Sunday School off and on as a boy but did not remember much. Moses was, apparently, the dude who spent forty years in the wilderness with the Hebrew people. Well, at least he knew who Jesus was. Everybody knew who Jesus was. At least they thought they did. He was the God dude born on Christmas Day. Right?

Feeling ignorant and eager to slip out of the embarrassing spotlight, Bob found his seat again and pulled the pointy elf hat over his face. Eric, sitting next to him on the train, put down his book and whispered, "Just face it, Bob, you're a rock star."

"Trust me, it's temporary," Bob answered.

Not Another Race of Creatures Bound on Other Journeys

"Maybe not," Eric was quick to challenge as he reopened his book.

Bob noticed this was a very old book with a cracked leather binding. Curious, Bob asked, "Any good?"

"The best," Eric said, "Dickens," and held up the cover of the old book for Bob to see. It was the classic, *A Christmas Carol*. "I read it every year. My father used to read it to me. Someday I hope I'll read it to my kids. Great story. Amazing writing. Listen to this. This is Scrooge's nephew speaking to Scrooge. This is good stuff."

And with great excitement, Eric read:

> *There are many things from which I might have derived good, by which I have not profited, I dare say . . . Christmas among the rest. But I am sure I have always thought of Christmas time, when it has come round apart from the veneration due to its sacred name and origin, if anything belonging to it can be apart from that—as a good time; a kind, forgiving, charitable, pleasant time; the only time I know of, in the long calendar of the year, when men and women seem by one consent to open their shut-up hearts freely, and to think of people below them as if they really were fellow-passengers to the grave, and not another race of creatures bound on other journeys. And therefore, uncle, though it has never put a scrap of gold or silver in my pocket, I believe that it has done me good, and will do me good; and I say, God bless it!*

Bob knew he was no angel, no shepherd, and certainly no Moses. But he also knew that some force beyond himself had taken hold of him that day, a force that had helped him, nay required him, to do things he would never ordinarily and under his own steam have done. Yes, it was the time of year, a good, kind, forgiving, and charitable time, as Dickens put it so well. But more than the blessed time of year had driven Bob. The very author of this and every time of year, the God of Moses, the God of angels, the God of Jesus, the God who had fashioned a band of blizzard-challenged strangers into fellow-passengers bound in one family, traveling on one journey.

The train pulled into South Station just about twenty minutes late, not bad at all. The older couple had reached Boston in time for the funeral. "I don't know how to thank you," the wife said to Bob, as she handed him a giant box of unopened chocolates that was undoubtedly intended for someone else. Bob tried to give it back but she insisted. The young woman who had almost traveled in a coach seat, stopped to thank Bob before hurrying off to the hospital where her mother lay so desperately ill. The woman with all the bells boldly hugged him before departing. The couple with the tiny baby added their thanks, as did the rest, to Bob's embarrassment and discomfort. Bob wished Eric a successful meeting with his fiancée's family, handed the box of chocolates to him, and asked him to find a good home for it. And off they went, each to his and her intended destination. Bob arrived home in time for the cancelled concert. His wonderful niece, Maddie, invited him to come over the next morning for a snowman making contest. How he adored Maddie and how grateful he was to his brother and sister-in-law for sharing their only child with him.

And in the days that followed, Bob attended to the Christmas list he had crafted on the train. There were six items on his list: 1. Find another home for the elf hat; 2. Update his professional clothing options; 3. Learn more about Moses; 4. Learn more about Jesus; 5. Purchase a copy of Dickens' *A Christmas Carol* and read it to Maddie as many years as she would allow it; and 6. Seek the sacred spirit that had gripped him so suddenly, opened his heart so freely, and bound him on an unexpected journey with an improbable assembly of fellow human creatures.

To you, O Lord, I lift up my soul. O my God, in you I trust;

do not let me be put to shame; do not let my enemies exult over me.

Do not let those who wait for you be put to shame;

let them be ashamed who are wantonly treacherous.

Make me to know your ways, O Lord; teach me your paths.

Lead me in your truth, and teach me, for you are the God of my salvation;

for you I wait all day long.

Be mindful of your mercy, O Lord, and of your steadfast love, for they have been from of old.

Do not remember the sins of my youth or my transgressions;

according to your steadfast love remember me, for your goodness' sake, O Lord!

Good and upright is the Lord; therefore he instructs sinners in the way.

He leads the humble in what is right, and teaches the humble his way.

All the paths of the Lord are steadfast love and faithfulness,

for those who keep his covenant and his decrees.

—Psalm 25:1–10, NRSV, A Reading for the First Sunday of Advent, Year C

9
A Humbled Heart

JAIME FOUND HERSELF ON a mission trip to Guatemala—by mistake. When her friends first started talking about it, it sounded like fun to a fifteen-year-old girl—shopping for bargains in a third-world marketplace, getting great deals on handbags and silver right before Christmas, eating exotic spicy foods, spending a week or so in an equatorial climate on a dreamy landscape of mountains and volcanoes. When her friend, Mike, asked her if she wanted to come along, Jaime had said, "Sure. I'll do that." But then she heard about the miserable poverty and the crime rate and the smog that made breathing in Guatemala City difficult. Apparently, the food was not all that exotic either, mostly variations of rice and black beans and an occasional chicken.

Jaime didn't like dirty places and she detested getting dirty or sweaty herself. But before she could bail out, Mike handed her the receipt for her plane ticket. With a big smile on his face, he said, "You're going to be grateful you did this." Jaime tried covertly to find someone to replace her, but the ticket was not transferable. She was the only person in the world who could use that airline ticket. When she discovered that the kids with whom they would be working often had lice and other parasites and that they would be working next to a putrid dump, she pleaded with her parents to let her stay home. Then, Jaime's neighbor told her she should not be going on such a trip because there were plenty of poor people in her own community and "Why would anyone spend all that money to go to another country to help the poor when people right here need that help!" Jaime was sure this neighbor was on to something. Immediately, she thought of a family nearby with only one TV, not even a flat-screen. This same dreadfully poor local family couldn't even afford a smart phone.

So Jaime gathered up all of her arguments and presented them systematically to her parents: the crime, the pollution, the stench, the disease, the beans, the "let's take care of our own poor" idea, and the "I'm not cut out for this dirty work" concept. She spread it all out before them and, surely, they would see what a mistake this trip would be for her. But, to her astonishment and frustration, they didn't buy it. Jaime's parents didn't cave this time because they were tired of their daughter's apparent inability to follow through on her promises. They were weary of the steady drip, drip, drip of self-centeredness she let fall on their heads daily. For the first time in a very long time, Jaime's parents put their feet down. End of story. No more discussion.

In fact, no one seemed to be interested in her opinions or complaints about the matter, not even Mr. Moody, Jaime's guidance counselor, who could always be counted on to listen. When Jaime presented him with her litany of objections to the mission trip with, of course, all the high drama that comes naturally to some fifteen-year-old girls, Mr. Moody simply let out a low contemplative, "Hmmm." He shook his head with what appeared to be disappointment.

Jaime must have looked as gloomy as she felt because Amanda Wilson, one of the few openly Christian students in the school, stopped and asked, "Are you alright?" Ordinarily, Jaime would not have given Amanda the time of day. Feeling, however, thoroughly ignored, she told her tale of Central American woe one more time as Amanda listened intently. When Jaime finally finished talking, Amanda said sincerely, "I'm going to pray about this situation." Jaime was surprised at her own gratitude for Amanda's offer. If prayer could possibly reverse her predicament, she was all for it.

The next day, Amanda handed Jaime a copy of the twenty-fifth Psalm. Two particular lines were highlighted. These lines were, "My God, in you I trust," and "God leads the humble in what

A Humbled Heart

is right, and teaches the humble the holy way." Now it was Jaime's turn to say, "Hmmm." She got the trust part right away. In fact, at this point, what else could she do but trust God? As for God leading the humble in what is right, what was Amanda trying to say? Was she trying to tell Jaime that she should lower herself? What she suggesting she do some sort of right thing?

There were four high school students on the mission trip to Guatemala and one chaperone, Mrs. Winklebaum, the Spanish teacher. Mrs. Winklebaum tended to give Spanish a New England twist, turning words like tortillas into tor-till-ers, and to give English a Spanish snap, turning words like window into ween-dow. The other three students didn't seem to mind the notion of thrusting their hands into the muck of Guatemalan poverty. And Mrs. Winklebaum couldn't wait to meet the niños hermosos, thee beaut-ee-ful cheel-dren. Jaime, however, her nails recently manicured, didn't want to do anything messy. She knew she didn't fit in with the others on the trip and was miserably aware of her bad attitude, but she simply couldn't help it. She knew she should care about the poor smudgy Guatemalan toddlers she had not yet met, but she really truly honest-to-God did not care.

The whole trip was looking like a bust for Jaime. The marketplace was not much fun because, if you stopped to look at anything, every weaver and flute-maker was all over you like ants on a candy car, to use one of her father's expressions. "I give you special price," they sang as if there were no other lyrics in Guatemala. She would have looked forward to relaxing in the hotel, but the electricity was undependable and the only shower she'd had was shockingly cold. Furthermore, she had been instructed to stay away from the water and not to eat anything that had been washed in it, which pretty much left the predictable menu—rice, beans, and chicken. Only two days into the mission trip, Jaime counted the hours until she could depart for home again. As she counted, she thought of all the things she was missing—the big Christmas sales in the mall, the annual festival of trees, opening day on the ski mountain. She was unalterably glum.

On the third day of the journey, the group traveled to the mission school where, at last, Jaime met the children she had been dreading. She did her very best to stay away from them, but they were persistent little creatures. In spite of her clear discouragement, they jumped on her legs, tugged at her T-shirt with their grubby little hands, and settled into her lap the minute she sat down. They didn't seem to mind that she didn't care one black bean about them.

These little rug rats were stinky and dirty and covered with scratches. Their clothes were long overdue for a laundering, many of their little heads had not seen a comb in days, and most of their ankles were flea-bitten. When she asked why their parents didn't simply give these kids a shower, she was told that many of these children live in shacks with neither running water nor electricity. When she asked about the bug bites, she was told that many live on dirt floors where they share a mattress with several sisters and brothers. When she asked why the government didn't do something about this, she was told the sad story of Guatemala, a story of ubiquitous corruption and a crippling gap between rich and poor. Jaime was genuinely and deeply shocked. She thought she had seen poverty, but poor people in her neighborhood didn't live in the abject squalor that surrounded so many of these big-eyed niños.

The mission group had brought a project along with them to work on with the littlest ones, an art project lovingly prepared by the creative high school art teacher. They were making crowns—coronas, and hats—sombreros. The crowns were made of thick paper cut into long strips with points cut along the top edge, the ends of the strips brought round to fit to each child's head. The sombreros were made of round cardboard with holes cut out of the middles so that the cardboard formed a brim around the top of each little head. Jaime noticed a tiny girl named Maria who gathered up all of the cardboard remnants that had been cut from the middle of the sombreros and silently wrapped them up in her filthy little jacket. "Why would she do such a thing?" Jaime asked. "Because her mother will sell that nice clean cardboard," came the reply. And that was the hallowed moment when Jaime's stubborn heart began to melt.

The kids quickly covered the crowns and sombreros with glue and glitter and buttons and feathers. Mrs. Winklebaum called it a royal dee-saster, but the kids seemed to enjoy themselves thoroughly and the whole cluttered event culminated in a colorful Christmas parade. Jaime found herself swept up in it all and, banishing the unhappiness from her humbled heart, she marched alongside everyone else in the makeshift parade. She carried a gleeful Maria in her arms, sparkly purple crowns adorning both of their lowly heads. She was abruptly and overwhelmingly grateful to be a part of such an unforgettably colorful world.

The parade of hand-crafted crowns and sombreros ended near a big wooden manger scene in the cafeteria of the mission school. There, as Jaime looked down into a roughhewn wooden cradle at a thoughtfully carved and beautifully painted café latte-skinned baby Jesus, and as she stared at the image of God purposefully humbled into human skin, the highlighted words of Psalm twenty-five came back to her as an unanticipated Christmas gift:

God leads the humble in what is right, and teaches the humble the holy way.

Jaime's life would never again be the same. Her understanding of the world had been turned inside out. The meaning of such words as 'poverty' and 'joy' and, yes, 'humble' were utterly transformed for her. The threshold of what is most important in this world was raised for her by those sweet tenacious little children to a previously unimagined level. And, while she would continue to get a French manicure from time to time, on this brief but soul-expanding mission trip, Jaime developed a life-long appreciation for the life-sustaining sweetness of rice and beans.

I thank my God every time I mention you in my prayers. I'm thankful for all of you every time I pray, and it's always a prayer full of joy. I'm glad because of the way you have been my partners in the ministry of the gospel from the time you first believed it until now. I'm sure about this: the one who started a good work in you will stay with you to complete the job by the day of Christ Jesus. I have good reason to think this way about all of you because I keep you in my heart. You are all my partners in God's grace, both during my time in prison and in the defense and support of the gospel. God is my witness that I feel affection for all of you with the compassion of Christ Jesus.

This is my prayer: that your love might become even more and more rich with knowledge and all kinds of insight. I pray this so that you will be able to decide what really matters and so you will be sincere and blameless on the day of Christ. I pray that you will then be filled with the fruit of righteousness, which comes from Jesus Christ, in order to give glory and praise to God.

—Philippians 1:3–11, CEB, A Reading for the Second Sunday of Advent, Year C

10
Finn's Feast

AARON FINNERTY, OR JUST plain Finn as everybody including his own children called him, looked forward to seeing his family as a thirsty traveler craves water. How grateful he was for his strange and wonderful quartet of kids. They were by no means perfect, but he was far from perfect himself and he knew this fact well. All planned to come for an early Christmas celebration, all four sons, Matthew, Mark, Luke, and John, lovingly named by his saintly wife, Jenny Lynn, may she rest in God's eternal peace.

Jenny Lynn had been the sparkling treasure of his life, and her strong kind mothering soul was carried away from this world when she was but forty-one years of age following a pneumonia that wouldn't let go. Finn, a long-standing member of the church and a big fan of Jesus, had never acquired Jenny's strength of faith. He longed to believe Jenny safely resided in the luminous realm of saints and of angels, but the only place he knew she surely rested was in his own heart and memory. She would always dwell in the home of his own modest soul, each remembrance of her bringing him ponderous joy.

After a few lonesome years, Finn had found himself a marvelous girlfriend and he loved dear Chloe fully and faithfully. But it would never, of course, be the same as the love he carried for Jenny, sweet Jenny, who had taught him the joy of marriage and generously borne him four remarkable children.

The boys were grown now. The eldest, Matthew, a computer whiz, had been scooped up by a Silicon Valley giant. Next in line,

Mark, a systems integrator, had taken a lucrative job in distant Dubai. Luke, a US Marine who, thankfully, survived three tours of duty in Afghanistan, now lived with his older brother, Matthew, in California while he figured out how to fit in to civilian life. John, the youngest and arguably liveliest of the bunch, had adopted the beautiful State of Montana as his home and become a proud ski bum. Not one of these boys was in a committed relationship or even had a steady partner to speak of. Luke had maintained an uneasy long-distance relationship for a while, but, when he came home from Afghanistan the last time, he ended it for good.

Finn wondered if their failure to thrive in relationship resulted from his own inadequate parenting, although the boys had reassured him many times that they were simply not ready to commit. In truth, Finn had never been a prize-winning father. He was not one of those super-dads who coaches little league, masters the scout troop, shows up to cheer at football games and helps with homework every night. Finn worked long challenging hours, and business had taken him away from home a fair bit. He simply wasn't around to do the heavy lifting when it came to parenting although Jenny had more than made up for his shortcomings. She had been the quintessential super-Mom—president of the PTA, Sunday School teacher, active member of the Boosters club, always ready to drive a pile of kids to the bowling alley. Jenny did it all.

Finn couldn't change the past, but he felt he had redeemed himself in recent years. Now partially retired with more discretionary time on his hands, he volunteered on the town architectural review board, coached middle school basketball, and took a class in Christian mysticism at the church. As the kids discovered his expanding extracurricular activities, they told Finn with enthusiasm how very proud of him they were. Imagine that! As proud as he was of them, whether he deserved it or not, they were proud of him, and he was inexpressively grateful for their support.

Finn considered their joint visit from far-flung locations a miracle of no small proportion. The prospect of his four sons coming home to sleep in their old rooms delighted him. Perhaps they would organize a Ping-Pong tournament as they used to do so often in the large game-room adjacent to the dining room. Their predictably playful conversation always came as music to his thankful ears. His heart filled with joyful expectation. Thomas Aquinas, one of his favorite new friends from the mystics class said, "Joy is a human being's noblest act." Aquinas also wrote, "The things that we love tell us what we are." That made a lot of sense to Finn for surely he knew who he was when he thought about those four amazing boys. From the moment of each birth, he had a deep sense that every child is truly a miracle. But, the older he grew and the more wisdom and insight he gained, the more blessed he felt to be a father.

The Finnerty house was spacious, beautiful, and curiously full of nooks, crannies, and unexpected spaces. A well-known inn at the turn of the 19th century, in its heyday, a few presidents and literary giants had graced its rooms. However, when the big motel chains moved into Vermont in the 1950s, inn-keeping fell on hard times. Finn and Jenny had purchased the inn for a song from his uncle and, together they made it home. Between his insurance business and some sound investing, Finn had done well for his family and could afford to heat and maintain the building. Their impressive historic home sat right on Main Street next to the General Store and across from the Community Church. The house had nine bedrooms, a huge kitchen, a walk-in pantry to rival Downton Abbey's, and a dining room with four chandeliers, remnants of a time when four large tables were seated with lively guests. In addition, the huge game room, always the favorite room of the boys, with both ping pong and pool tables, carefully maintained, and a beautiful antique octagonal card table from the Victorian era impressed visitors.

Finn anticipated a great family feast in the big dining room. He looked forward to drinking in the lively banter among his boys. He was eager to embrace them, to feel their muscular warm backs in his palms. Chloe, who had a knack for such things, had helped decorate the dining room. A large festive display of fruit sat in the middle of one table and she had set out the good China, the cloth napkins, the family silver. It would be a feast set for kings.

The menu, however, caused a bit of a problem. Finn had spent days wondering what in the world to serve at this glorious mid-December homecoming feast. What menu might meet everyone's dietary peculiarities? Matthew had gone gluten-free and Luke, who could be a bit of a monkey-see monkey-do brother, seemed to be falling in line with his big brother. That ruled out anything with stuffing, and it ruled out cake. Mark had gone vegan with the surprising exception of bacon, which was apparently hard to find in Dubai. John, on the other hand, was a happy Montana hunter presently sporting a Paleo diet which consisted mostly of meat, the gamier the better. So, some of his boys ate meat; some didn't it; some ate wheat, some didn't. What was a father to do?

Eventually, Finn decided on variety as the path of greatest inclusion. He bought the biggest roast beef he could find, two large turkeys, five pounds of thick-cut locally smoked bacon, a dozen acorn squash, four dozen farm-fresh eggs, twenty pounds of white potatoes, and three pounds of sharp Vermont cheddar. He also bought five pounds of crisp green beans to top with sliced almonds, ten pounds of sweet potatoes, five pounds of red onions, several large containers of mixed nuts, a huge bag of frozen jumbo shrimp, a gallon of whole milk, and a gallon of almond milk. From the local bakery, he ordered an apple pie, a chocolate cream pie, a pumpkin pie, a blueberry pie, and two pecan pies, his personal favorite. His girlfriend, Chloe, would make her own fresh vanilla bean ice cream and thick whipped cream. Pie or no pie, everybody loved Chloe's ice cream. Finn's aimed to set out such an assortment of food, it would be a satisfying feast for everyone. He realized he had bought far too much food, probably enough to feed the whole town if need be, but he would rather have too much than too little and no one enjoyed leftovers as well as Aaron Finnerty.

Busy preparing and enjoying his own happy anticipation, he had failed to monitor the forecast. Snow in Vermont in the middle of December is not unusual but, suddenly, Finn tuned into a predicted multi-day monster storm about to descend upon New England just as his kids were getting ready to travel. Meteorologists anticipated three to four feet of fresh snow. Now, Finn could be a worrier and, upon digesting this unpleasant news, he found himself consumed by concern for his four boys who were supposed to be flying in from three different directions. They had carefully arranged their flights to arrive in Boston within a couple of hours of one another. From there, they would rent a car and drive up Route 89 together. Based on the forecasts, however, the airport might be closed and driving could be treacherous.

With some heart-felt reluctance, Finn sent out an email to the boys apprising them of the situation and instructing them not to take any chances. He wanted them, first and foremost, to play it safe. The boys told him they would play it by ear, watch the weather, and see what was possible. Mark was the most reluctant because traveling more than twenty hours from Dubai only to be diverted to some place like Atlanta because Logan airport was closed. The trip seemed more of a risk than he was willing to take. Finn understood. He was, of course, disappointed but the well-being of his boys was what really mattered. He supposed, however, that he should go ahead and prepare the feast just in case any of them did manage to show up. John was the most likely to show up because of his utter fearlessness. John relished snow and drove in any and all conditions.

On the morning of the day the boys were due to arrive, with a blizzard building and more than a foot of fresh snow on the ground already, Finn and Chloe began to cook. When they lost power, they kept going. A large brick fireplace in the kitchen with warming shelves on the side and a gas stove that was not dependent upon electricity saved the day. Lovely old glass oil lanterns and four wood stoves lit and warmed the house. He and Chloe didn't miss a step as they prepared the turkeys, the stuffing, and the roast, created au gratin potatoes, and cranked out one dish after another. Finn had always enjoyed cooking, a passion he shared with Chloe. They spent hours in the kitchen that morning, channeling his worry into savory productivity as snow continued to blow into mountainous drifts.

By late morning, they hadn't heard from any of the boys, and the feast was looking bleaker and bleaker. When Logan airport officially shut down, that confirmed the whole disappointing matter. Finn tried to call the boys but nobody answered. He suspected the storm was interfering with calls, and he hoped and prayed they were all okay. Then, after a while, he began to feel selfish. He should have put his foot down and instructed them, in no uncertain terms, not to come. On a good day, he would be anxious about them all being in the air at the same time, but now his concern nearly overwhelmed him. But then he remembered St. Aquinas, who preached, "If the highest aim of a captain were to preserve his ship, he would keep it in port forever." Whether the boys had stayed in their respective ports or not was out of his hands. At noontime, he heard from John and was thankful beyond measure. John had made it as far as Philadelphia, just below the storm line, and would probably spend the night there in a hotel. Furthermore, John had received text messages early that morning from Matthew who was, along with Luke, stuck in sun-drenched California where the airline could not assure a window into Boston. No one had heard from Mark. Finn and John assumed, however, that he had wisely stayed put in balmy but bacon-less Dubai.

Finn asked Chloe what they might do with all that food since the boys would not be coming after all. What could they do with the big juicy roast, the perfectly browning turkeys, the giant tray of apple and sausage stuffed acorn squash, the huge casserole of creamy cheesy potatoes, the pecan-topped sweet potato dish, the shrimp, the beans, the pies, the ice cream. Chloe suggested that the Thompson family down the street might appreciate being invited for a hot dinner. Everyone knew the Thompsons were good eaters. That sounded like a fine idea to Finn, who recalled Aquinas saying something to the effect that our material possessions are not our own and are to be shared without hesitation.

The Thompsons were so pleased by the invitation, they told a few neighbors about the feast, who told a few others and before Finn could say, "There's no more room in the Inn!" Finn and Chloe had thirty-five neighbors coming for dinner. Thank heavens for the large dining room. In the thrill of the moment, it occurred to Finn that, if they expanded the meal into the game room, there would be room for even more. A dependable old pot-belly stove heated the game room nicely, and the ping pong table alone could seat twenty. They placed a piece of plywood covered with a tablecloth over the pool table to fashion a buffet table. Finn stoked the stove while Chloe set up the buffet. Together, they brought in chairs from other rooms and put a few shiny fragrant McIntosh apples in the center of each table.

At about 5:30, the Thompsons showed up with a squash casserole, followed by the Sweeneys with a pungent venison stew. Rev. Albert Morris from the church across the street brought a pound of fair-trade coffee and another pecan pie (can there ever be too much pecan pie?), the Martins brought four loaves of warm crusty bread and a pound of butter, and the Bessettes carried in a large pot of corn chowder. Jugs of apple cider lined the buffet and people who'd survived such storms before carried in five-gallon buckets of water for flushing. A spontaneous parade of snow boots, food, and good wishes brought the old inn to life again. More than sixty neighbors, old and young, showed up for the feast and had plenty to eat with plenty to spare. Marnie and Ella Young busted out their fiddles and people sang out Christmas Carols and tapped their toes in the diffused glowing light of the oil lamps while, outside, frosty wind made moan. No one noticed the lack of power; they had plenty of their own.

Now, there is a lot to be said for big cities that sparkle 24/7 with concerts and shows, fusion restaurants and world-class museums. But there is nothing like a small town. There is nothing quite like the cooperation, the collaboration, the kindness, and the care that can permeate a small town, melting away worries the way snowflakes disappear into warm hands. There is nothing like the acceptance that is possible when neighbors know one another's imperfections and idiosyncrasies as well as they do in day-to-day village life.

As the night wore on, no one being particularly anxious to leave the revelry and fellowship, Rev. Morris, never at a loss for words, lifted a toast to Finn and Chloe. Well aware of Finn's growing appreciation for St. Thomas Aquinas, he said, "Magnanimity is the expansion of the soul to great things. Here's to Chloe and Finn and the great things they have done today!" Following a round of approving applause, he then summoned the gathering to prayer, saying: "Holy One, we thank you for the joy we celebrate in this place, for the neighbors we love in this place, and for the compassion and grace we share in this place. May your love continue to abound among us. We thank you that there was room for you and for everyone in the inn tonight. And bless, O God, Finn's sons that they may be safe and sound wherever they are. Give light to all who sit in darkness, guide our feet in the way of peace and receive our thanks for every blessing."

Before the good Reverend could tack on a satisfactory "Amen", an icy blast came from the main foyer. In walked John out of the blustering night, followed by Luke, Matthew, and finally, Mark. John had rented the biggest heaviest all-wheel drive vehicle available, had driven up to Newark airport where the others had managed to land safely. Together, the four had carefully made their way up to Vermont, following plows much of the way.

Although plenty of good hot food remained, the boys chose to dive into the pies. Forks in hand, they were pleased to see what a hero their father truly was. Finn, the master of the feast, hugged those boys tight, had an extra helping of gratitude, and was as full as a man can be.

Surely God is my salvation; I will trust, and will not be afraid,

for the Lord God is my strength and my might; he has become my salvation.

With joy you will draw water from the wells of salvation.

And you will say in that day: Give thanks to the Lord, call on his name;

make known his deeds among the nations. Proclaim that his name is exalted.

Sing praises to the Lord, for he has done gloriously; let this be known in all the earth.

Shout aloud and sing for joy, O royal Zion, for great in your midst is the Holy One of Israel.

—Isaiah 12:2–6, NRSV, A Reading for the Third Sunday of Advent, Year C

Rejoice in the Lord always; again I will say, Rejoice. Let your gentleness be known to everyone. The Lord is near. Do not worry about anything, but in everything by prayer and supplication with thanksgiving let your requests be made known to God. And the peace of God, which surpasses all understanding, will guard your hearts and your minds in Christ Jesus.

—Philippians 4:4–7, NRSV, A Reading for the Third Sunday of Advent, Year C

11
The Gift of the Maggies

MAGGIE'S MOTHER WAS AFRAID that a simple stop at the nursing home would turn into an hour-long burden. She often wondered how it happened that a mother as quiet and reserved as she could end up with a child as forthcoming and outgoing as her little Maggie. There were so many things Maggie's mother needed to get done that Sunday afternoon. She still had Christmas shopping to finish and a tree to find, and Maggie kept asking for electric candles in the windows this year. She had hoped to bake cookies, and single moms simply don't have any help with such matters. They have to keep going no matter what. Maggie, however, all six years of her, had stubbornly insisted on going to the nursing home. All of the children of the Sunday school had made angel ornaments out of white tissue paper and silver glitter, each one as unique as its creator, for delivery to shut-ins. Maggie didn't care how much time it took. She wanted "in" on the hand-made gift giving experience.

In a divinely random distribution of assignments, Maggie was asked to deliver her little angel to Mrs. Margaret Dearborn. Maggie and her mother did not know Mrs. Margaret Dearborn and had never before visited the local nursing home. Little Maggie seemed to have enough spunk and determination for both of them, so off they went after church to participate in "Operation Angel Drop-Off".

The nursing home sparkled with symbols of the season—wreaths on the windows, a crèche at the nurses' station, a small artificial tree in one corner of the activity room. A nurse at the front desk pointed out Mrs. Dearborn, seated by herself at a small square table. Mrs. Dearborn was reading a newspaper with a big magnifying glass. Mrs. Dearborn's small size impressed Maggie. Maggie remembered her own Grandmother, who had died just last year, as quite a tall woman with straight dark grey hair. Petite Mrs. Dearborn had curly white hair and lustrous blue eyes. Maggie thought she looked sort of like a retired angel. "Hello," said Maggie brightly, forwarding the sparkly ornament in the direction of the woman.

"Well, what have we here?" the woman asked extending a small, frail hand to examine the unexpected gift.

"It has two sides," offered Maggie, rotating the angel so that Mrs. Dearborn could see that on one side the angel was smiling and on the other side, she was singing. "I think angels are supposed to sing," Maggie said, as if offering a bit of expertise on the subject.

"That's what I understand." Mrs. Dearborn replied, then added, "I'm a little hard of hearing. Did you say what your name is?" Maggie's mother stepped in and said, "I'm so sorry, Mrs. Dearborn, we should have introduced ourselves. This is Maggie and I'm Maggie's mother, Marianne. We're visitors from the church."

"It is a pleasure to meet you. To what do I owe the honor?"

"Oh, you don't owe me anything," Maggie said. "We're just supposed to give you the angel. It's free."

Ever so gently, Maggie's mother, squatting down to face her gregarious daughter, said, "Maggie, Mrs. Dearborn wasn't asking if she owes you anything. It's an expression. 'To what do I owe the honor?' is a very polite way of asking us why we're here."

"Oh, I get it," Maggie said. "It's like 'full of baloney' doesn't really mean you're, you know 'full of baloney.'" As she said this, Maggie looked at Mrs. Dearborn and stuck out her belly, rubbing her little hands around the middle of it to demonstrate what might be mistaken for 'full of baloney.'

"Something like that," Mrs. Dearborn responded sweetly.

The Gift of the Maggies

"Do you like her?" Maggie asked, pointing to the angel that now sat atop the green and blue plaid blanket on Mrs. Dearborn's lap.

"I like her very much, thank you," the white-haired woman in the wheelchair said, "and do you know something else?"

"What?" Maggie asked, looking as if she might burst if she didn't find out.

"My first name is Margaret and when I was a little girl, my parents called me Maggie too."

"No!" Maggie exclaimed loudly and with evident astonishment.

"I wouldn't kid about something like this. We are both Maggies."

"Isn't that something," Maggie's mother said.

"Remarkable," added Mrs. Dearborn. Maggie's mother could see that people were being wheeled away, presumably to lunch. A quick escape, she thought. She was thinking that the timing of their visit was really perfect because, nice as Mrs. Dearborn truly was, she would soon be summoned to the dining room and they could be on their way—on to the imperative tasks of the season. She thought about shopping first, perhaps running down to Sherman's Bookstore for a nice calendar to send to her brother in Colorado and looking in Calypso's Clothing store for a soft sweater for her boss. Her mind wandered to ten other places when Mrs. Dearborn's invitation brought it racing back into the nursing home. "Maggie, would you and your mother like to stay for lunch? We're having chicken soup and tuna sandwiches today."

Maggie's mother, anxious about how much she had planned to squeeze into the day ahead, jumped in quickly in order to avert any extension of the visit. She said, "We have quite a busy afternoon, and I'm sure the kitchen staff has plenty of people to feed today without adding unexpected company." Maggie, however, never shy about her own preferences, started a plaintive, "Please, please, please, Mom, please." And what could Maggie's mother do but resign herself to the moment?

97

O'er All The Weary World

Over lunch, the Maggies discussed such things as school, homework, how much snow might fall before Christmas, how both Maggies were learning to use the computer, how both liked tuna fish without onion chopped up in it and how both loved snicker-doodle cookies dunked in cold milk. Marianne listened considerately and tried not to stare at the big round clock on the wall that whispered insistently of the lateness of the hour and the number of responsibilities she was shirking. She anticipated a very busy stretch of time at work, and Maggie seemed to have some special event after school every day this week. Marianne wondered where would she find all the time for these motherly tasks and finish getting ready for Christmas, while attending to the demands of work.

Mrs. Dearborn had brought the angel ornament to the table with her. As the soup bowls and sandwich plates were cleared, young Maggie picked up the ornament again and asked, "Have you ever heard an angel sing? I haven't but I'd like to."

"I don't think so." Mrs. Dearborn went on to talk about the wonderful church choir and how she wished she could get there to hear it. She hoped the church would soon get a sound system so that recordings of the morning worship services might be shared with people like her, stuck inside most Sunday mornings.

"Yeah, we have a really good choir," little Maggie said, feeling both proud of her church and sad that Mrs. Dearborn couldn't hear the singing. But then she had an idea. "*I* could sing for you!" Maggie announced excitedly.

"Maggie, Mrs. Dearborn must have other things to do this afternoon," Marianne said. Other nursing home residents had been listening to their conversation all along and were all shaking their heads in unison as if to make it perfectly clear—not only did Mrs. Dearborn have no other plans; none of them had any plans. A woman sitting across the room piped up, "I'll play the piano for you," pointing to a neglected upright in the corner. So much enthusiasm in the room for the impromptu concert persuaded Marianne to stay a little longer. She said, "Just a couple of songs, Maggie. Then we need to give these kind folks back their afternoon." Heads were shaking again, reminding Maggie's mother that her agenda would not carry the vote around here.

The volunteer accompanist shuffled over to the piano and asked, "Do you know, *Away in a Manger*?"

"Of course," Maggie answered, almost defensively, as if to say, "Who doesn't know *Away in a Manger*?"

Maggie's surprisingly strong voice belted out the hymn with little finesse but boundless spirit. And, of course, *Away in a Manger* was only the beginning. Everybody requested a favorite Christmas Carol, and Maggie was eager to sing every one, whether she knew them or not. It was obvious that Maggie was making up some of the words, but no one seemed to care. This feisty little girl and her fearless rejoicing enchanted them.

And then something interesting happened. Maggie's mother, caught up in the joy of the moment, forgot about the tree, the cookies, the shopping, the decorating and the other very real but perhaps unnecessary stresses of her life. When the concert ended with a stirring rendition of *Angels We Have Heard On High*, every nursing home resident adding his or her voice to the big 'glorias,' Marianne suddenly felt ready for Christmas. She was thankful for her wonderfully determined child, and she felt an inexplicable peace.

Mrs. Dearborn thanked Marianne and Maggie for visiting and invited them to come again soon. Marianne thanked Mrs. Dearborn for lunch and for such a lovely afternoon. Just as they were leaving, as Maggie stood at the door waving 'Goodbye', Mrs. Dearborn motioned Maggie to come back. She held up the little angel ornament and whispered, "You know, Maggie, I think I have heard an angel sing today."

Therefore, when he comes into the world he says,

You didn't want a sacrifice or an offering, but you prepared a body for me; you weren't pleased with entirely burned offerings or a sin offering. So then I said, "Look, I've come to do your will, God. This has been written about me in the scroll."

He says above, You didn't want and you weren't pleased with a sacrifice or an offering or with entirely burned offerings or a purification offering, *which are offered because the Law requires them. Then he said,* Look, I've come to do your will. *He puts an end to the first to establish the second. We have been made holy by God's will through the offering of Jesus Christ's body once for all.*

—Hebrews 10:5–10, CEB, A Reading for the Fourth Sunday of Advent, Year C

12
Everybody's Got an Angle *or* Everybody's Got an Angel

ALICE LOVED HER STUDIO. She climbed the dramatically wide oak steps up to her painting studio almost every day for more than forty years. Alice bought the old white cape out on the point overlooking the ever-changing ocean the year she turned forty. That year, her artwork took off in the public eye and she gained widespread recognition as a brilliant painter of sea and sky. As mentioned, that was now more than forty years ago. You can do the math, but what the math doesn't tell you is that eighty-two is the new sixty-two. Nothing about Alice was old. She still played a mean game of tennis. She was still a formidable force around a bridge table. She embodied a skepticism that was as fresh as this morning's Op Ed page. And Alice had no trouble with her daily pilgrimage up the oak steps to her beloved studio.

Alice's dog, Max, was sadly another matter. Max was now fourteen and quite arthritic. He used to climb those steps with her every day and curl up in a shady spot in the summer, a sunny one in the winter. He kept Alice company the way no other creature on earth could.. Max was, in fact, the only creature on earth she trusted. Her neighbors always seemed to want something from her. Her friends were sometimes undependable. But Max? Max was always right there for her—half black lab, half mystery dog, all wonderful. Alice wished Max could be up here with her now as she sat still, feeling cantankerous and alone, alone in the big comfortably messy studio that, once upon a time, had been an attic.

When Alice purchased the house, it was thoroughly run down but structurally solid. With the help of a talented local builder, she transformed the attic into a temple of luminosity. Light streamed into the studio at different angles all day long—east to west with limited southern exposure but scads of soft northern light to indulge her canvasses. All of Alice's paintings were huge but never large enough, she felt, to scratch the surface of her understanding of the subject. And all of Alice's paintings were colorful, like Alice. Her current project depicted a twilight seascape in which the line between heaven and earth, the line between a silent sky and a still ocean was indistinguishable, the stars above reflecting on the dark salty deep. The painting was developing nicely, she thought.

Alice stroked the tip of a small horsehair brush with her index finger wondering if she could muster the energy to make a little progress on the painting. But she could not. It was Christmas Eve, after all, and Alice was too grumpy to paint, too grumpy and too lonesome. She imagined people all over town gathered in homes or churches, toasting one another or teasing themselves with the notion of a God who descends to earth in self-sacrificial love. Ridiculous. Alice let herself fall back into a plump wing chair that had acquired its own color palate after years of sitting in the same room with so much paint. She slumped into the now form-fitting chair and allowed cynical seasonal thoughts to swirl inside her head.

One of her favorite movies was *White Christmas* because she identified with the generation that produced Rosemary Clooney and Vera-Ellen. The line from *White Christmas* that kept returning to her as an unbidden mantra was, "Everybody's got an angle." Bing Crosby looked into the eyes of the lovely young Clooney and said, "Everybody's got an angle." He was so right, reflected Alice. Everybody's got an angle. They're all out for themselves, she thought. One of her neighbors had brought over some fudge but asked, at the same time, if she might contribute a painting to the community auction. Bah! Church carolers offered a stirring

Everybody's Got an Angle or Everybody's Got an Angel

rendition of *We Three Kings* even as they dropped off a fund-raising brochure. Humbug! Because Christmas was, apparently, a time for gratuitous pulling on heartstrings as well as purse-strings, every day her mailbox filled with plump with requests for charitable donations. Phooey. On a grander scale, the merciless machines of violence, genocide, and global warming kept grinding away, fueled by greed, lust for power, unexamined hatred, unadulterated selfishness. Awful!

Everybody was out there greasing somebody else's palm trying to get whatever it is they wanted for themselves. Bing Crosby was right—everybody's got an angle. Why God would ever come down to a place like this and sacrifice anything to the kind of nonsense with which the world busied itself was beyond Alice. As she sat transfixed by her ruminations, caught between the evening beauty just beyond the studio windows and the bleakness spinning in her mind, she heard a slow familiar clomping. It was Max, the rough pads of his feet with their tough nails hitting the hard oak steps. A low canine grunt accompanied each footfall.

Walking was hard enough for the old dog, but climbing steps was torture. She called out to him, "You don't have to come up here, Max," but he kept coming nevertheless. Slowly, agonizingly, one paw at a time, he made his way to the top of the steps and to her grateful side. "Max, old Max," she said lovingly, scratching behind his ears with both hands. She looked into his big droopy brown eyes and spoke to her beloved companion, "You don't have an angle, do you Max. There is nothing up here for you. Nothing at all. No tennis balls. No food. You came up here just because you love me and you're willing to sit here with crabby old me." His sacrificial climb put the sacred back into the season and made her feel almost shockingly holy.

Looking out the big north window of her studio, the magnificent stars, her current subject matter, looked somehow brighter than ever. They whispered to her of a God who, like Max, might just get bundled up and come down to earth for no other reason than an irrational love for the earth's creatures and a sacrificial willingness to sit with humanity in its various states of sin, discontent, and common crabbiness. "Hmmm, could be," Alice thought aloud. She turned to Max, her furry old angel and, allowing a small bud of faith to bloom in her heart, she peered back out in the heavens where the line between the silent star-studded sky and the deep still ocean was nearly indistinguishable. Then she winked at God, and with a bit more conviction in her voice, proclaimed, "Could be."

Now the birth of Jesus the Messiah took place in this way. When his mother Mary had been engaged to Joseph, but before they lived together, she was found to be with child from the Holy Spirit. Her husband Joseph, being a righteous man and unwilling to expose her to public disgrace, planned to dismiss her quietly. But just when he had resolved to do this, an angel of the Lord appeared to him in a dream and said, "Joseph, son of David, do not be afraid to take Mary as your wife, for the child conceived in her is from the Holy Spirit. She will bear a son, and you are to name him Jesus, for he will save his people from their sins." All this took place to fulfill what had been spoken by the Lord through the prophet:

"Look, the virgin shall conceive and bear a son, and they shall name him Emmanuel," which means, "God is with us."

—Matthew 1:18–23, NRSV, Traditional Reading
 for Christmas

13
It Is What It Is

MADELINE STRATTON KNEW CHRISTMAS would be challenging this year. No one was coming home. Oh, she understood. She completely understood that her kids and grandkids wanted to wake up in their own homes with their own families on Christmas Day. She thoroughly appreciated that everyone had to work and that they were all fortunate to have jobs. Their work schedules precluded the long drive home to see her, and it would be formidably expensive for everyone to fly home. Both of her children, Kate and David, had invited her to visit them for Christmas but, of course, she had to work too and didn't have any vacation time. "It is what it is," she reminded herself.

Madeline determined, however, to make hers a meaningful Christmas. If the holiday couldn't be fun and family, well then, at the very least it could be meaningful. She would, of course, prefer both fun *and* meaningful but she would settle for meaningful. It is what it is. And so she looked for acts of kindness. It was a year in which people were being more deliberate about kindness and "paying it forward," and Madeline was happy to be a part of the movement. In response to the unspeakable school shootings in Connecticut, some folks aimed for acts of kindness. She wondered how many kindnesses she could enact before Christmas. She would do what she could. The world desperately needed less violence and more kindness, less sorrow and more love.

As her first effort, Madeline selected four gift tags from the community gift tree and enthusiastically shopped after work. The shopping list was simple enough, or so it seemed: a large hoodie sweatshirt for a sixteen-year-old boy, a fashion doll of any kind for an eight-year-old girl; a pair of boots, preferably black, size seven, for a fifteen-year-old girl, and some ear buds for a ten-year-old boy. She decided to travel to one of the big department stores with one of those thirty percent off coupons that make you feel as if you've saved more than you've spent.

It felt wonderful to go shopping for these kids, whoever they were, and she admirably avoided shopping for herself (always a temptation). A shimmery holly-green sweater on the sale rack that was almost too good to pass up tempted her because it was an eighty-nine dollar sweater marked down to fifteen dollars. With an additional thirty percent off, the cost reduced to ten dollars. At that rate, they were practically paying her to shop, but she held her ground. She was not there for herself.

Picking out the hoodie proved more difficult than she anticipated. Zipper or no zipper? Dark or light? NFL or NBA? She wished she could dismiss the choices and just grab "whatever" because the kid should just be grateful he's getting anything at all, right? But that was not how she felt. She wanted this young man to be happy with her choice. She selected a soft gray name-brand hoodie and held it out in front of her to study it. It is what it is. If he hates it, he can simply exchange it, right?

The fashion doll was easy. There was a very beautiful sparkly Christmas doll with a dark red velvet dress trimmed in faux diamonds. What little girl wouldn't want that? Heck! She was tempted to buy one for herself but, again, she resisted valiantly. The black boots were a little challenging but, praise God, she met a Mom shopping for boots for her own teenage daughter at the same time. Following an impromptu conversation about this year's fashion footwear preferences, Madeline selected the same brand and type of boot that the younger Mom had picked and set off to find electronics. Ear buds. She figured, "How hard can ear buds be?" But there were so many colors—neons, patterns—and so many different ear tip configurations; some were noise isolating and some were not. Finally, she chose the most comfortable looking ones in basic black with the more expensive noise-isolating feature and called it good.

The best part, of course, is that, when she finished shopping, the receipt indicated she had spent $82.14 and had saved $203.76. What a rush! But, of course, once she had delivered the wrapped gifts to the community Christmas tree, twelve days more days remained until Christmas. She needed to find another act of kindness to lend meaning to her Christmas.

She had read that the Sunday School children were raising funds for the Children's Hospital and thought of helping them out by soliciting funds from her neighbors. This turned out to be a brilliant idea. To begin with, she enjoyed visiting with her neighbors—it had been some time. She gathered all sorts of information about them which she might otherwise never have learned. For instance, Mel Parker had just come home from the hospital. How had she missed that one? The McLeans were preparing for all five children plus spouses, significant others, and grandchildren to arrive for Christmas—seventeen in all. Madeline felt exhausted just thinking about it. Sitting with her neighbors, picking up tidbits here and there, pleased her and everyone inquired as to her Christmas plans. She wangled an invitation to Christmas dinner at the McLeans. When you're having seventeen, what's one more? They planned to serve prime rib. She couldn't remember the last time she'd had a juicy delicious prime rib. More importantly, when she'd finished, she'd raised one-hundred and twenty-three dollars to add to the Sunday School fundraiser. That was wonderful. She added twenty-seven of her own dollars, writing a check for $150, all for the Children's Hospital. How's that for meaningful?

But nine days remained until Christmas. Although her work kept her very busy during the day, she was acutely aware that, by about 10:00 p.m. on Christmas Eve, she would start facing thirty-hour hours of home alone. She'd better find some more kindness and meaning to fill the time, or Christmas, except for the prime rib of course, would be pretty empty. As Christmas Day approached, "It is what it is" became less and less assuring.

Madeline knew a community luncheon would take place soon, part of a free lunch program organized by the churches. While she couldn't be there to serve due to her work schedule, she could make a hearty soup and maybe a few cookies. And so, she did. One evening, she baked chocolate chip cookies and the next evening, she made magic cookie bars (who can resist those?) On the third evening, the night before the luncheon, she made a nice thick cheeseburger soup. She dropped the food off at the church on her way to work. While there, she signed up to read at the 8 p.m. Christmas Eve service. It wasn't exactly an act of kindness but what could be more meaningful than reading scripture on Christmas Eve?

What next? What other acts of kindness could Madeline complete? She thought of the nursing homes. There were two nursing homes in town, the fancy one already decorated to the hilt and the sort-of-run-down one that probably was not. She could volunteer to decorate. Why, she owned enough Christmas "stuff" in the basement to decorate 3 or 4 nursing homes! She had no interest in decorating her own home this year but bringing some festive touches to others could be fun.

Sure enough, the sort-of-run-down nursing home staff would be delighted with a few more decorations! Madeline spent one evening sorting through containers in the basement, deciding what she could donate. She spent the following evening at the nursing home, quietly stringing garland, setting up a few window candles, and using a dusty corner table to display an old incomplete crèche. The only figurine was the baby Jesus, but would these nursing home residents even notice?

But they did notice. Most of the residents were already tucked into bed, but two men in wheelchairs had wordlessly watched her the whole time. Suddenly they piped up when it looked like she had finished, saying, "Hey, where's Jesus?"

"I don't know," Madeline answered honestly while she pretended to scour the bottom of the empty shopping bag from which the incomplete holy family had emerged. "It is what it is," she said to them but that was clearly a most unsatisfactory answer. No baby

Jesus. She wondered where she could find just a baby Jesus. Nobody sells just a baby Jesus, do they?

"It ain't right," one of the men preached. The other one responded, "Oh, don't listen to him. That baby isn't even supposed to show up until Christmas, right? Don't you worry about him. You just come back on Christmas with that little baby Jesus, OK? You can stay for our Christmas supper too if you want. We're having hamburgers."

"And tater tots," the grouchy one added.

"And Boston cream pie, don't forget the Boston cream pie," added the first one.

Well, the nursing home visit had not quite worked out as she'd planned. The whole experience had the unanticipated and certainly undesirable effect of making her feel rather cheap. Rattled by the whole encounter, Madeline slept poorly that night. In a disconcerting dream, she found herself *in* the nativity. A tall angel pointed to the empty manger. When she looked down into the manger, however, she found it was not empty at all. And here's the really weird part of the dream—*she* was the one in the manger. Lonely old Madeline was the one found lying in a manger.

The next morning Madeline, still shaken by the dream, gave up her pursuit of kindness and meaning. What had she been thinking? What could she really do anyway? Instead of trying to manufacture things to do, she returned to what she should have been doing from the start. Madeline packed up the gifts for David and Kate and their families, gifts she had been semi-deliberately ignoring and lugged them to the post office. Then she got out the boxes of Christmas cards and spent several evenings composing one Christmas card after another.

On the morning of Christmas Eve, she received an email reminder about her reading that night. In the first chapter of Matthew, her assigned verses told of an angel appearing to Joseph in a dream. A chill ran up her spine as she recalled her own dream. Having practiced her reading, Madeline arrived at church early enough to sit contemplatively for a minute. The church looked beautiful, as it always did at Christmas, with fresh wreaths on the windows and a big aromatic tree in the corner. On the communion table sat a lovely old crèche with all the pieces, including the babe in the manger. She sighed. It is what it is.

The congregation sang the usual Christmas carols, but they did not feel as bright as she felt they should have. Was the organist unusually sluggish or did her own attitude mute their joy? Then they sang *In the Bleak Midwinter*, which she never liked; why would anyone pick such a dreary song to sing at such a time? This year, however, as she listened to the words, they felt strangely appropriate. "What can I give him, poor as I am?" she sang, thinking of the feeble acts of kindness she had offered this season. This hymn grew on her. And then she read her lesson, treasuring the word 'Emmanuel' that shone like a jewel within it, and she sat back down.

The minister's homily was, as usual, a bit dry, with lofty quotes here and there. But one of those quotes stuck in her head and started swimming around like a goldfish in a bowl that is too small. Meister Eckhart[1], wrote, "We are all meant to be mothers of God, for God is always needing to be born." And in the revelatory glow of these words, she viewed her efforts over the past few weeks from a completely different perspective. If God was at work in her, if God was being born in her again as she chose gifts tags from the community tree, searched for the right gifts to put with those tags, listened to her neighbors share the details of their lives, raised a little money for a good cause, made her cookies and cheeseburger soup, and even as she tried to brighten up the somewhat dilapidated nursing home, then she truly was the babe in the manger, just as her strange dream had suggested.

She knew in that moment that the meaning of Christmas is not to be found in the gifts themselves nor in the time she'd given to them nor in how they had made her feel. The meaning was in God working through her as she had done each task. Christmas was not about Madeline Stratton or anything she could or couldn't do or any act of kindness she got right or did not get right. This

---

1. Meister Eckhart, a German philosopher and theologian, who lived from 1260–1327, was one of the great Christian Mystics.

was about God born into the world, born into human hearts even the likes of hers. This was about that mysterious birth process in Meister Eckhart's writings. *This* is what it is!

Christmas morning was quiet but not especially sad, more in a lovely *Away in a Manger* sort of way. She did not feel as terribly alone as she had originally feared she might. With a fresh determination, she went sorting through her craft boxes filled with string and buttons and fabric. All she found that could possibly be fashioned into a baby Jesus were some little white yarn puff balls. She glued three of these together, turning them into something like a miniature snowman. Then, she wrapped the puff balls in a small square of royal blue felt and added two dark peering eyes with the fine tip of a permanent marker. "It is what it is," she thought, staring at her tiny creation, adding, "This is what it is."

With apologies to the McLeans who had so kindly invited Madeline to share their holiday prime rib, she gussied herself up in a bright red sweater, took the freshly swaddled puff balls, and returned to the nursing home. There, to the delight of the residents, some of whom had been wondering when Jesus was going to show up, she hung up her coat and placed the puff-ball infant in the manger. With the sweet meaning of Emmanuel at rest in her soul, Madeline proceeded to play a rousing game of Bingo with the residents and to stay for a Christmas supper of hamburgers, tater tots, and Boston cream pie.

Bear one another's burdens, and in this way you will fulfill the law of Christ. For if those who are nothing think they are something, they deceive themselves. All must test their own work; then that work, rather than their neighbor's work, will become a cause for pride. For all must carry their own loads. Those who are taught the word must share in all good things with their teacher.

Do not be deceived; God is not mocked, for you reap whatever you sow. If you sow to your own flesh, you will reap corruption from the flesh; but if you sow to the Spirit, you will reap eternal life from the Spirit. So let us not grow weary in doing what is right, for we will reap at harvest time, if we do not give up. So then, whenever we have an opportunity, let us work for the good of all, and especially for those of the family of faith.

—Galatians 6:2–10, NRSV, Not a Traditional Advent Reading

14
O'er All the Weary World

KEVIN STOOD OUTSIDE, THE warmth of strong sun gripping his dark green T-Shirt. The colors of Spanish and Mayan heritage adorned a steady stream of pedestrians; the sounds of street vendors and poorly tuned trucks resounded in his ears; the smell of the vast Guatemala City dump numbed his nasal passages. Kevin held an unopened card tightly in his fist, its vivid red envelope broadcasting the Christmas card inside. The bright card was from his parents.

Kevin was young to be so far from home and on his own for the first time. He turned eighteen in July, one month after graduating from high school. To his dismay and embarrassment, Kevin had not been accepted into his first college choice (which shall remain nameless), nor his second or third (which shall also remain nameless). He wondered what sort of brainiac superhero a kid had to be to get into a good college these days.

His "back up school" accepted him (small consolation), but he decided quite stubbornly, almost petulantly, that he would not attend a school that took nearly everybody. Why his back-up school (which, in all fairness, shall remain nameless too) even took Allie Wilmer who, as far as Kevin could tell, had somehow made it through high school without ever cracking a book. The regrettable situation forced Kevin to reopen his youthful options. He could work for a year and try again. He could apply for a mid-year acceptance into another college. His father, true to his industrious nature, wanted him to get a job. "If you're not goin' to school, Hero, you'd better get to work." Kevin hated when his father called him Hero.

His father also sometimes called him a "Do-Gooder", which Kevin found to be equally offensive. "You're such a do-gooder, Kev," his father would say, eyes narrowing, brow furrowing in perplexity. Well, what was wrong with doing good? Kevin wanted to know, although he didn't dare question his father. In such instances, his mother would usually whisper, "Don't mind your Dad. He means well. He's awfully proud of you, Kevin." After a modest pause, she would add, "Really," as if adding the word 'really' had the power to make it so.

Most of the time Kevin felt like a great disappointment to his father, who had set a football in his hands as soon as he was big enough to hold one. Kevin, to the dismay of his big brawny father, was always and to this day a little small and scrawny for football and was not, by nature, especially athletically inclined. Kevin's father, a master woodworker, had made most of the furniture in the house and encouraged Kevin to follow in his carpentry footsteps. But Kevin's fine motor skills never seemed adequate work.

Kevin had his own gifts, however, and he tried very hard to please his father. He would never be a celebrated athlete but he did enjoy running as a member of the track and field team. The best he could do for the team was not trip over his own feet and, at most meets, struggle his way bravely to the middle of the pack. His peers respected him, nonetheless, and, in his junior year, he received the coach's "Heart" award. Kevin also excelled in academics, even if the top three college choices (which shall continue to remain nameless) had rejected him.

What Kevin enjoyed, most was helping others. He had probably volunteered more than any other student in his high school. He delivered mail and magazines to patients in the local hospital. He collected gifts and coats for poor children at Christmastime. He sheet-rocked for Habitat for Humanity. He raised money for disaster relief. He volunteered to help first and second graders in the elementary school with their reading. He taught the pre-school Sunday School Class at his church. If anybody needed a hand,

Kevin was the first to raise his. He was no "Hero" as his father called him with that almost mocking edge that drove Kevin crazy; he just loved helping other people.

His post High School 'Plan B' deliberations led him into a volunteer opportunity, a decision that surprised no one, including his parents. Kevin had asked his minister for ideas, and she suggested an educational program in Guatemala called *Safe Passage*[1] that welcomes long-term volunteers. Their motto was "Combating Poverty Through Education". Kevin liked that. The job did not offer a salary but would give him the chance to make a difference in the world as well as an opportunity to contemplate his future.

At age eighteen, Kevin was the youngest long-term volunteer at *Safe Passage*. In her letter of recommendation, his pastor had boasted that Kevin was "wise beyond his years," but he did not always feel so wise. In fact, he was sure he had said something dumb or done something stupid every day since his arrival in Guatemala City late in August. His pastor had also written, "Kevin never grows weary in well-doing." When he'd asked her about that particular turn of phrase, she'd told him to look it up in the third chapter of Second Thessalonians. When he did he found St. Paul's timeless admonition to disciples of Jesus: "Do not grow weary in well-doing."

Do not grow weary in well-doing. Those are nice words but the truth was that Kevin grew weary all the time. He grew weary of trying to understand the fast-moving Spanish that flew by his ears all day long. He grew weary of his own inadequacies and blunders. He grew weary of the inequities that surrounded him—the extraordinary wealth of a few and the deadly poverty of the many. And he grew weary just thinking about the fact that he went back to a small but reasonably comfortable bed every night while the children with whom he worked sometimes slept on the smelly dirt.

His volunteer job at *Safe Passage* was to teach English to the children. Kevin's Spanish was shaky at best but the kids didn't seem

---

1. Safe Passage is an education mission that serves poor children and their families who live in the vicinity of the dump in Guatemala City. For more information, visit: www.safepassage.org.

to mind. Most of the time, he played games with them using flash cards and pictures and bean bags. His first day on the job terrified him, but the large dark eyes and sweet laughter of the little children in his classes washed away any fear. Most of the time, he did feel like he was making a difference, opening doors of knowledge to some of the poorest of the poor children of the world.

Kevin learned he never could have learned in any of those exclusive schools that had refused him. But Guatemala proved a lonely place for him. He longed for a friend his own age, maybe even a girlfriend. A couple of months ago, a group of very cute girls from the States had volunteered at *Safe Passage* for a week. Kevin yearned for them to stay longer. He had wished they might remain long enough to notice the good heart behind his often awkward presentation. But that hadn't happened.

He thought about his Mom and Dad often but had not experienced any serious homesickness until recently. Kevin supposed this had something to do with the coming of Christmas. At the beginning of December, if he'd stayed home, he would now be hoping for snow and getting involved in collecting toys and coats for needy children. Christmas in Maine is a special time, and Guatemala is at least a world away. He would never need a heavy coat here. In Guatemala, a T-Shirt sufficed almost all the time—all year long. He found himself missing the change of seasons, the way a warm fire feels on a raw day and his mother's winter stew.

Kevin would not be home for Christmas this year. He would celebrate with a few of the other volunteers and try not to miss his own home too terribly. He knew his parents missed him, especially his mother. He felt certain that she understood what he was trying to do and felt equally certain that his father did not.

Kevin had shopped for his parents' Christmas gifts in the artisans' market. He found a striking quilted carry-bag for his mother, crafted by local weavers in the vibrant rainbow colors that are so characteristic of Guatemala. For his father, he found a pocketknife with a Quetzal, the colorful, long-plumed national bird of Guatemala, carved into its wooden casing. He would wrap these gifts soon and ship them home.

He told his parents that he really didn't want anything for Christmas this year. Opening gifts when most of the children around the dump would not be opening anything on Christmas morning would have felt uncomfortable. Instead of presents, he encouraged his parents to send a donation to *Safe Passage*. That is what he bravely informed them. A secretly wishful part of himself, a part not so wise beyond his years, hoped they would send something anyway, a small gift he might unwrap in the solitude of his room on Christmas morning. The red envelope was probably, however, the biggest gift that would sit under his imaginary tree this year. He wanted desperately to open the card still clutched in his hand. Twenty-two days remained until Christmas, but he wanted to tear into the envelope and hear from his parents. Instead he stuffed it into his backpack and headed for his next class.

The children in his late morning class were learning animal names and Kevin had brought with him a cloth draw-string bag filled with small plastic animals. "Buenos Dias," he greeted the children with a big smile on his face. "Buenos Dias," came the delightful sing-song reply. Each child reached into the drawstring bag and pulled out an animal. Some of them were pleased with their selections; others were visibly disappointed. For some reason, nobody ever wanted to be the goat. The snake, on the other hand, always seemed to be a lucky draw. No matter. They would choose again tomorrow. Each child was encouraged to say the name of the selected animal in Spanish and in English. Caballo—Horse. Gato—Cat. Serpiente—Snake. Cabra—Goat. They played animal musical chairs. They sang Old McDonald in Spanish and in English. They laughed. They had fun. They learned. He learned.

After class, Kevin went next door to the cafeteria to get some rice and beans for lunch. His mother, who rarely cooked with beans because she knew how much Kevin disliked them, would have been astonished at the quantity of beans he had consumed in the few months he'd been in Guatemala. As Kevin sat chewing his rice and beans, he pulled the card out of his backpack and stared at it once more. Clearly, his mother had addressed the card, her beautiful round script nearly a work of art. How he missed her gentle reassuring voice and how he missed her cooking! Finishing his lunch, Kevin tossed out the thoroughly emptied paper plate, throwing out all patience and maturity with it. He tore open the envelope.

Bright silvery angels hovering over an image of the earth in splendid blues and greens on the Christmas card cover. On this little card, the distance between Guatemala and Maine was very small indeed. Below the beautiful earth were the words, "And still their heavenly music floats o'er all the weary world." Kevin loved the thought of holy angels watching over a world weary of corruption, a world weary of greed, a world weary of brutality, blessed angels moving us closer to goodness and peace. He opened the card. He had fully expected all the writing to be from his mother but much to his surprise, it was his father who had written inside the card. His father. The printed greeting inside the card read: "May God fill the whole world with heavenly peace." In his father's jagged handwriting were these thoughts:

"Dear Kevin, I'm full of pride over what you're doing down there. When I was your age I don't think I would have been so brave. Your Mom and I are sending a check to 'Safe Passage' for Christmas. Whatever happens, Kevin, don't ever get tired of doing good things. Merry Christmas. Love, Dad and Mom"

Brave. His father thought him brave. Kevin felt warm inside in a way that had nothing to do with the weather or the beans. Why, it was almost as if those beautiful angels on the front of the card had suddenly dive-bombed from their divinely appointed posts pouring heavenly music over all the weary world. These welcome angels climbed inside his fatigued chest, filling him with fresh energy and banishing all loneliness, all homesickness, all inadequacy. And that line about not ever getting tired of doing good things! Why his father, whether he knew it or not, was practically quoting the Bible where it says: "Don't grow weary in well-doing."

This message was better than any funny little gift Kevin might have opened on December twenty-fifth. Why he might even re-wrap the card so he could open it again and feel the warmth afresh on Christmas morning. In that moment, every bit of sticky rejection Kevin had experienced in the year past evaporated. In that moment, every bit of awkwardness vanished. In that moment, Kevin felt completely and thoroughly blessed. And, as he headed to his next class, he was ready again to share the blessing with others.

In those days Caesar Augustus declared that everyone throughout the empire should be enrolled in the tax lists. This first enrollment occurred when Quirinius governed Syria. Everyone went to their own cities to be enrolled. Since Joseph belonged to David's house and family line, he went up from the city of Nazareth in Galilee to David's city, called Bethlehem, in Judea. He went to be enrolled together with Mary, who was promised to him in marriage and who was pregnant. While they were there, the time came for Mary to have her baby. She gave birth to her firstborn child, a son, wrapped him snugly, and laid him in a manger, because there was no place for them in the guestroom.

Nearby shepherds were living in the fields, guarding their sheep at night. The Lord's angel stood before them, the Lord's glory shone around them, and they were terrified. The angel said, "Don't be afraid! Look! I bring good news to you—wonderful, joyous news for all people. Your savior is born today in David's city. He is Christ the Lord. This is a sign for you: you will find a newborn baby wrapped snugly and lying in a manger." Suddenly a great assembly of the heavenly forces was with the angel praising God. They said, "Glory to God in heaven, and on earth peace among those whom he favors." When the angels returned to heaven, the shepherds said to each other, "Let's go right now to Bethlehem and see what's happened. Let's confirm what the Lord has revealed to us." They went quickly and found Mary and Joseph, and the baby lying in the manger. When they saw this, they reported what they had been told about this child. Everyone who heard it was amazed at what the shepherds told them. Mary committed these things to memory and considered them carefully. The shepherds returned home, glorifying and praising God for all they had heard and seen. Everything happened just as they had been told.

—Luke 2:1–20, CEB, Traditional Reading
   for Christmas Eve

15
Eben's Angel

A Children's Story for Christmas Eve

This is a mostly true story about a boy who is really named Eben and who really picked out a tree-top angel the year the church misplaced its tree-top star.

Participatory suggestion: If read aloud, children listening may be invited to flap their arms like angels wings whenever they hear the word 'angel' and to wiggle their fingers in the air as if they are shining whenever they hear the word 'star'.

EVERY YEAR, IN THE weeks before Christmas, a fresh evergreen tree arrived at the church. A star used to sit on the very tippy top of the tree as a reminder of the one that shone so brightly 2000 years ago on the town of Bethlehem, the star that led the wise men to the baby Jesus. One year, nobody could find the star that for so many years shone dependably from the top of the church Christmas tree. The decorating committee looked in every closet and every cabinet and every storage bin in the church. They even looked all the way up in the belfry in the church bell tower, the last place anybody wanted to look because it was so mouse-ridden and dark, but they could not find the star.

And so that year, a boy named Eben who was then thirteen years old, volunteered to go into the village to find a new star for the church Christmas tree. He found the village busy and the people anxious as they picked things off the store shelves. Eben knew they were all trying to get ready for Christmas, and he was happy that he was getting the church ready for Christmas. In one store, he discovered a few tinselly stars that did not look like they would last. In fact, they did not look very much like stars to him. In another shop, he found a fancy electric star with a bright light inside that would have been very impressive indeed. But he could not imagine putting a phony-looking electric star on the handsomely natural tree. He also saw a big beautiful glass star, but it was the kind that hangs in a window, not the kind that nestles on top of a tree.

While Eben looked for just the right star, an interesting thing happened; he found just the right angel. On the top shelf of a village shop, a lovely angel seemed to be looking right at him. She was pearly gold with lacy wings and a flowing gown. The beautiful angel made Eben feel calm inside, the way you feel when everything is right and good in your life. She looked just the way Eben always imagined an angel should look. She was not a star, but she did shine like a star, and Eben thought he could hear her whispering, "Take me with you."

Eben paid for the angel and took her back to the church where a small group of children and grown-ups were putting the last string of lights on the huge freshly cut fir tree. When they saw the bag in Eben's hand, they couldn't wait to see the star he had purchased to top the tree. With a big smile on his face, Eben carefully took the beautiful angel out of the bag and showed her off to them all. They didn't say anything. Not one person spoke. They just stared at his magnificent angel until one little girl finally said, "Eben, that's not a star." She sounded a little disappointed and upset.

"I know she's not a star but she's going to look perfect on the tree."

Just then, the minister walked in and said, "We can have an angel on the tree. A star on the tree is very special because it reminds us of the bright star of Bethlehem that led the wise men to where Jesus was born. But an angel on the tree is also very special. She reminds us of the angel who announced the birth of Jesus to the shepherds."

Eben was holding the angel very carefully, the way one holds something important.

"But," said one of the adults to the minister, "we've always had a star. I grew up in this church, and I can't remember anything but a star."

Eben started to feel funny about the whole thing and he stared at his angel. She seemed to be looking back at him as if to say, "Don't be afraid," for that is very often what angels say. They say things like, "Fear not. Don't be afraid."

The minister spoke again, saying, "Not everything can always be the way it used to be. We'll keep looking for the star, but let's put the angel on top of the tree and let's see how it looks."

Eben felt a little better. The minister took the angel from him and handed it to a grown-up named Mr. Pinkham who was standing on a ladder holding a long stick. Mr. Pinkham put the angel on the stick and tried to place her on top of the tree. But the tree was very big and tall that year, and the angel wobbled as he tried to reach the top branch. She fell off the stick and onto the floor. Eben raced to pick up the angel and was relieved to see she wasn't broken. She was fine. There was not even a scratch on her.

Mr. Pinkham, the man on the ladder, put the angel back on the stick and tried again to place her on top of the very tall Christmas tree. Once again, she wobbled and fell off, but this time Eben was ready and caught her gently in his hands.

The same little girl who was so upset yelled out, "See? That angel doesn't even want to be on our tree. You should have bought a star."

"It's not the angel's fault," said Mr. Pinkham, "this tree is so big, I need a taller ladder! Let me try one more time, Eben."

He handed Mr. Pinkham the angel, and Eben worried that this angel would never make it to the top of the tree. But this time, when the man lifted her up near the top branches, she seemed to jump up off the stick to the tippy top all by herself. And just like that, there she was, shining perfectly from the very top of the tree. She looked like she was singing to everyone, "Peace on earth," for that is another thing angels do. They announce peace and goodwill on earth.

And in that moment, Eben felt nothing but peace and goodwill toward everyone, even the little girl who gave him such a hard time about not finding a star. He remembered the people he saw in the stores buying gifts anxiously. He had bought only one thing—a beautiful angel for the church tree—and yet Eben felt completely at peace inside, completely ready for Christmas, completely ready for God to be born again into the world.

And the minister took a Bible out of a pew rack and read from the second chapter of the Gospel according to Luke:

> *Nearby shepherds were living in the fields, guarding their sheep at night. The Lord's angel stood before them, the Lord's glory shone around them, and they were terrified. The angel said, "Don't be afraid! Look! I bring good news to you—wonderful, joyous news for all people. Your savior is born today in David's city. He is Christ the Lord. This is a sign for you: you will find a newborn baby wrapped snugly and lying in a manger." Suddenly a great assembly of the heavenly forces was with the angel praising God. They said, "Glory to God in heaven, and on earth peace . . ."*[1]

---

1. Common English Bible.

www.ingramcontent.com/pod-product-compliance
Lightning Source LLC
Chambersburg PA
CBHW050831160426
43192CB00010B/1979